Additional Reviews

The murder mystery in the new novel, *Dealing Out Death*, keeps the reader guessing until the end. The tale is about the dark side of addiction and the affect it has on the family and friends of the aflicted. Written by a daughter at the request of her mother who lived and died addicted to gambling. The author tells a poignant story backed by a lot of truth. The murder investigation unfolds the truth a layer at a time, building up to the revealing of the killer. I couldn't stop reading this book. I enjoyed it immensely.

Danna J. Walters, Author
Gaze Upon A Blue Moon

Though on the surface, Jo A. Wilkins's new novel, *Dealing Out Death*, appears to be a cautionary tale for gamblers, a closer look reveals more. It soon becomes a compassionate story of the family and friends caught in the wreckage of an unrestrained addict. The writing is smooth and well-paced; the characters vivid and sympathetic. A definite recommendation.

Stephanie Cress, Author
Gilded Shadows

DEALING

OUT

DEATH

Jo A. Wilkins

Ink & Quill Publishing

Henderson, Nevada
2018

Dealing Out Death
Jo A. Wilkins
Copyright © 2018
All rights reserved

Line/Content Editor: Janelle Evans
Interior Design: Sara Walsh
Cover: Richard Draude
Patch on Cover purchased from: www.ebay.com/str/ MILTACUSA?

p. cm. — Jo A. Wilkins (Mystery — Copyright © 2018 /Jo A. Wilkins
All Rights Reserved
ISBN: 978-1-948266-02-4/Paperback
ISBN: 978-1-948266-35-2/E-Pub

1. Fiction/Myatery & Detective/General
2. Self-Help/Substance Abuse/General
3. Family Relationships/Disfunctional Family

www.iqpublishers.com

Henderson, NV 89002
Printed in the United States of America

1 2 3 4 5 6 7 8 9 10

This book is dedicated to my mother, Conchetta (Connie) Esterline.

Her dying wish, two weeks before her death from stomach cancer, was for me to write this so others would know, how her gambling addiction had ruined her life and affected her family.

DEALING
OUT
DEATH

CHAPTER
1

WAKE UP CALL

"**A**nnie." Shelli touched my shoulder and I bolted up.

"Have they found her?" I looked around my bedroom hugging my shoulders against the shiver threatening to shake my core, exhaustion begging me to go back to sleep.

My cousin's whole body sagged and she shook her head. She glanced away, but not quick enough to hide the misery we shared.

Ignoring the steel bands gripping my stomach, I threw off the afghan covering my legs. "Your job as a nurse may teach you to shield your feelings behind your uniform, but you're not wearing it now. I've known you since you were born and I know that look. You may be able to fool Dane with it, but not me."

Shelli's shoulders slumped even further. "They'll find her soon. I know they will." She walked away, pacing the floor at the foot of my bed. Her long, straight black, Asian-looking hair swished across the center of her back—so out of place in this Italian family of ours—but her grandfather hailed from the Philippines. She stopped in front of the closet and fiddled with the door, sliding it the last few inches I hadn't bothered with to close it. Such motherly concern, although, at twenty-seven, she was five years younger than me.

I pushed the sarcastic thought away. For years Shelli—the daughter of my oldest cousin—had been the younger sister I had always longed for. "She's been gone too long, Shelli. And you know my mother as well as I do. She never goes anywhere without my father. And have you ever known her to leave the

1

house for more than ten minutes without calling someone in the family?" With a family as big as ours there were plenty to choose from.

Her eyebrows shot up.

"Okay, except when she drags Dad to a casino. But then, he's there with her—isn't he!"

"But I know they'll find her," Shelli said, with less conviction than before. "My dad and brother, Uncle Joe, and Uncle Dolly are still out looking for her with your dad. Uncle Wayne has the search well organized."

"Yes, my Dad's years on the police force left him very methodical." I let out a faint snicker. "I guess he had to, to stay a step ahead of Mom all this time."

I swung my legs over the side of my bed and rested my forehead in the palms of my hands. When my fingers moved through my limper-than-usual dishwater brown hair, I feared looking into the mirror over my dresser because Mom's high cheekbones and slender nose would stare back at me. The only differences in our looks were my green eyes and the thin, brown, cottony hair, so like my fathers.

I tried again to straighten the strands with my fingers but hearing an increase of noise coming up the hall, I stood. "Are there more of them in the living room?"

"Some in the kitchen too, now. They haven't started cooking yet, if that's any consolation." A smirk filled her face. "But I suspect they will pretty soon.

How many of our Italian family had gathered in the other rooms of my house waiting for news about Mom while I slept?

Shelli paced the floor again. "Annie, I know she's been gone longer than usual, but I don't see why you're so sure we won't find her."

"Shut the door."

She crossed the room and peeked into the hall before easing the door back into the latch.

"I don't want whoever is in the other room to hear us but I need to tell you about the argument Mom and Dad had yesterday. I went to their apartment in the afternoon to check on when or if

2

they were coming over for dinner. I found their apartment empty and walked through the hall leading into the manager's office. I was just about to go inside when their argument leached out through the open door. I couldn't believe what they said to each other. I don't think I've heard my father that angry since he left the police force.

"I stayed behind the partition. You know, the one that hides the entrance to the office from their apartment. It was dark in the hall, so they couldn't have seen me through the latticework. I didn't interrupt them, 'cause I hate it when they suck me into their arguments. I backed up when Mom headed for the hall. She came right at me until he grabbed for her purse.

"At first," I said looking past Shelli's astonished expression, "I thought she had seen me, and I almost went inside. I thought they were ignoring me, 'cause they just kept yelling at each other."

"Are you sure they didn't see you?"

"I don't think so. Anyway, I ducked farther back into the hallway just in case. I stayed there just long enough to know she's in a lot of trouble this time."

"Dad accused her of stealing the rent monies." I touched Shelli's arm. "He told her he wouldn't be part of her *thieving* anymore. Then, he said that if she didn't replace the money she took—right away—he'd turn her in to their boss and let her go to jail."

Shelli glanced down at the rug. "I can't believe she's taking the money from the rents they collect. What'd she say when he threatened to turn her in?"

"You know my mother—she laughed! She told him she'd always replaced the rent money before. That this apartment complex was no different than any other they had managed, and she had everything under control."

My hoarse voice rang in my ears. "Shelli, even with all the money she borrows from the family, she's been *stealing* from the places they've worked. She told Dad she just needed one big win to make everything right.

"He yelled at her, in a harsher tone than I ever remember him using. His shout echoed off the walls and I was afraid someone

3

outside might hear them. He said she hadn't just borrowed five or ten dollars or even fifty dollars this time. She had taken over four thousand dollars from the till — *Four thousand dollars!*"

Sitting on the foot of my bed, I resisted the urge to plant my head back onto the palms my hands. "I've always known she gambled and borrowed lots of money from everyone." I stared up at Shelli. "But I never suspected she'd steal to pay for her gambling."

Shelli's stricken look mirrored my emotions last night standing in that empty hallway, listening to that fight.

"But... I know we'll find her, Annie," she said again. "The whole family is out there looking for her. And now that we know how bad her problem is, we can tell everyone. We can find help for her."

"I don't think the family wanted to see it — *I* didn't want to see it." I rubbed my temples to clear away the exhaustion creeping into my mind. "I just can't shake the feeling that something bad has happened to her. You know her — Dad has to be with her all the time, and she's been gone by herself for..." I glanced at the clock. "...fifteen hours!"

For the first time since last night, Shelli smiled. "Yeah, what is it my brother always says?" She deepened and ruffed up her voice to sound like Lewie. "Auntie can't take a dump without knowing Uncle Wayne's standing just outside the bathroom door."

When I couldn't muster enough energy to return her smile, her shoulders sagged again.

"I've got to get back out and look for her." I stood, my growing fears for my missing mother made it impossible to stay here any longer. "Someone must have seen her — someone must know where she is. Yes, she sounded irrational but this isn't like her — not at *all* like her."

Shelli and I both glanced at the closed door when loud laughter came from the living room. *Could she be home?*

We hurried out into the hall.

Almost at the end of the hall, I winced at Saunta's comment. "I'll bet this is another of my cousin's stunts to get attention."

4

The laughter stopped when Shelli and I reached the edge of the living room rug.

My grandmother, Nana, sat in the rocker, surrounded by two of my aunts. Saunta had planted herself among the ten or so others in my living room. Shelli's mother, Rosalie, coordinated the cooking that had started in the kitchen.

Do other Italian families turn to cooking when faced with family problems?

Uncle Vince, the only man in the living room, lowered the footrest of the recliner at my entrance. He said nothing, but the apprehension in his expression as he leaned over and shared a whisper with Nana was impossible to miss. Everyone else in the room remained quiet.

Aunt Carmen jumped up, filling the silence. "Here, Annie, take my seat."

My feet responded to her offer of their own accord. I left Shelli's side avoiding the faces of the people who had helped shape my life. "Where's Uncle Joe?" I asked Aunt Carmen, more to hear noise than to have an answer.

"He's still out with your dad, looking for your mother," she whispered.

I took her seat on the couch trying to smile, but I'd had all I could take of the sneer on Saunta's face. It needed to be dealt with. "I see you made it out your front door again, Saunta. Did Aunt Sis bring you over today?"

My words hit their mark. Her agoraphobic nature surfaced and a timid, scared-of-the-world look took over until she muttered something under her breath.

Her face hardened again. "I came here like everyone else — to support you with the family until Mama-Doll decides to come home. I think your mother is being horribly inconsiderate to everyone by disappearing like this." She turned to the others in the room. "You remember when she —"

"Saunta!" Uncle Vince said before her usual tirade against my mother gained more steam.

Why was Saunta even here? She and Mom fought every time they saw each other. Neither of them had managed to outgrow their childhood jealousies of one another.

Uncle Vince raised the footrest but again avoided my eyes. "I hate it when my gout flares up," he said hitting the side of his leg with his cane. "Saunta, I think we should center our concern on the disappearance of my sister." His soft voice and teddy-bearish looks didn't hide his stern attitude.

"I think we should all look at the positive side of this," Aunt Sis said standing next to the divider separating the living room from the dining room and kitchen.

Nana cleared her throat.

I glanced at Nana, the aged matriarch of the Capriccio family, along with everyone else. She leaned forward in the rocking chair I kept in my house just for her. Her soft, wrinkled features shined under her short, curly gray hair. Nothing in the world calmed me more than that beautiful face.

"It'd be nice if ya'll would think about how we can help my daughter, instead-a thinking bad thoughts 'bout her." She wrung her hands together in her lap.

The only time Nana didn't speak in soft tones was when her Sicilian temper flared. The soothing flow of her voice held everyone's attention, but I fixated on the movement of her hands. Oh, those small, gentle hands. Nana stood an imposing five-foot-ten-and-a-half inches, but any touch from her delicate hands always came as a caress.

"Are ya alright, child?" Nana said me in her half Italian accent, half Louisiana drawl. "I told them t' keep it down and not t' wake ya. Ya need your rest after bein' out all night looking for my *sstupido e imprudente* daughter."

"I'm alright, Nana." I rose from the couch and sank cross-legged on the floor next to the rocker. "Did they make any progress finding Mom while I slept?"

Nana shook her head. She reached out and patted my hand resting on the arm of the rocking chair. "All will be okay," she whispered. "Ya wait and see. She'll turn up."

"Who's still out looking for her?" I asked to everyone in the room.

"Well, Joe's still out," Aunt Carmen said. "But the others are on their way back in."

"Why?"

"Because we've looked in all her usual places," Dad said.

I glanced up to see him standing just inside the front door.

He spoke to Aunt Carmen. "Joe's gone ahead to check out some of the casinos near the Strip, and Dolly and Big Lewie wanted to search downtown before heading back here."

He looked at me with eyes sadder than I'd ever seen on him. "Annie, I have to meet your Uncle Joe back at the Continental in half-an-hour, but I had to check on you."

My father, more in command than I'd seen in years, made his way across the room. In the midst of questions shouted from every corner of the living room and dining room, he came straight to Nana's side. He reached down, pulled me up, and gathered me into his arms. On my back, I felt Nana grasp his hand for a short squeeze.

The noise that is my family never quieted while Nana and I comforted Dad. He released me from his hug and I turned to find ten more people crowded into the living room. Some peeking through the three-post, half-wall divider between the two rooms.

"We have no idea where she's gone," my dad told them all. "But I doubt Mama-Doll has left town. We just haven't found her anywhere."

Uncle Vince stood with the aid of his cane. He passed us on his way to the kitchen, saying, "Well, you'll need to eat something before you go back out."

Aunt Sis and Shelli followed him into the other, now less crowded, room of my house.

Dad sat down, taking Aunt Sis's place on the loveseat. His strong German features wilted, though he still held that determined look I saw on his face when he entered the house.

"You've been out searching for my daughter since last night," Nana said, "you must be starved."

At another mention of food, I envisioned Mom, as she would have been, in the middle of my kitchen showing everyone a better way to put the meal together. But, as I listened to the chatter around me, Mom and Dad's fight from last night echoed in my ears. They had continued their fight from the office in this very living room. Here, they hadn't cared that my neighbors or I might hear their words.

They must have forgotten where they were, and I tried not to listen. Although, an argument that loud is hard to ignore. He had called her a *crook*! I had laughed so hard that I stumbled, with the salad in my hands, on the way to the dinner table.

Dad hadn't stood up to Mom for so long I still couldn't believe his words. For the last few years, he just grumbled when she went on a rampage and headed for the other side of the room to sulk, but in the end, he would follow, or take her wherever she wanted to go.

I hated seeing the loss of the quiet strength he used to have. I guess in the fifteen years since he'd left the LAPD, being under Mom's thumb 24 hours a day had taken its toll.

Emulating the worried look on Dad's face, Nana settled back in her chair. "My daughter's strong—she'll come back okay. It's her hard-headed attitude that's ru'nin' her life. We've all seen her getting' worse over the years. But, lately, she's been 'specially foolish."

"Yeah," Saunta said chuckling. "If Mama-Doll is around when you're cooking and you lay down a spoon on the stove—you know, so you could stir the pot a little later—she washes the blasted spoon. She'll even throw away the napkin it rests on. And she'll do it before you take more than one step away from the stove. She..."

A look from Dad turned off Saunta's prattle.

During that second fight last night everything had come apart. He'd lost it after Mom told him *again* he had no business questioning how she handled money. He vowed never to go to a casino with her, ever again. By the tone of his voice even I recognized that he meant it. When he chucked his keys at her, hitting the wall near my front door and yelled that he wouldn't be going home with her either, I worried about them. Then he added, in such a soft voice I almost missed it, that from now on he'd be staying at my house—without her.

Mom picked up the keys and stormed out the front door and

no one had seen or heard from her since!

Aunt Sis entered the living room and handed Dad a plate holding a sandwich and a few slices of apple. "After you eat this, Wayne, I'm going back out with you. If my sister hasn't got the courtesy to let us know where she's been for so long, I want to be there when you find her. I'll knock her off the slot machine stool I know she's sitting on all by myself."

"Me too," said Saunta, but I knew better. "I can't wait. Maybe we can make up for that train ride from Newhall to L.A. where we missed our chance when we were kids."

I moaned inside. I had heard that old story a thousand times. Even now, under these circumstances, it filled me with the hopeless task of trying to defend my mother to her brothers, sisters.

"Steffi," Saunta said turning Aunt Sis, "you remember how your father found out that we planned to throw his eight-year-old spoiled brat off the train on our Saturday shopping trip into Los Angeles?" She looked around at the silent faces in the room. "We had it all figured out, didn't we? How we would lure her out onto the back platform and get rid of her and that uppity attitude once and for all."

Saunta turned from Aunt Carmen's stern look to face Aunt Sis, determined to have her say.

"If your father hadn't found out and made her sit right next to him for the entire train ride, we would have been rid of her whining back then."

She glanced around the room, looking for support.

"You all remember. That's when Connie got her nickname, Mama-Doll, because Uncle Vincent treated her like his little China doll."

Nana hush her niece with a sharp glance. "That happened in the past, and right now, we should be more interested in findin' my daughter than in dredgin' up old stories 'bout her."

At the half smile that crossed Aunt Sis's lips when she turned back into the kitchen I realized that not one of them, except for Nana, Dad, and me, feared that Mom had gotten herself into real trouble this time.

CHAPTER 2

SEARCHING

*L*eading **Shelli through the casino,** the smoke and noise assaulted my nose and eyes. I pressed my phone closer to my ear, trying to mute the bells and whistles of nearby machines. "Yes, Aunt Sis. We spoke to an employee named Elsie. She saw Mom here at Western Town last night. I also found another lady, a Marion Eastman, who remembers seeing her here around midnight. She told us Mom won a twelve-hundred-dollar jackpot on a royal flush."

"Did that lady...wh...she..."

"What?" I said raising my voice over the pop and sputter the phone made in my ear.

"...di...ho...sh...say...ho...long...bef...you —"

"What did you say? You're breaking up badly."

"...wh...di...sh...g...after her win?"

"Aunt Sis, if you can hear me, I'll call you back when I get outside."

I snapped my phone shut and waited for Shelli to catch up. We headed for the nearest exit. From the corner of my eye I watched the younger, skinnier of the two men who had followed us for the last fifteen minutes. He pulled on the arm of the good-looking older fellow with him at our change of direction. They trailed us all the way to the side exit. Out on the sidewalk, I urged Shelli around behind a group of people waiting by a bench for their rides.

The two men — security, I hoped — rushed outside after us. The younger one looked around in a panic. The other glanced

11

at the bench full of tourists a couple of times before he saw me sitting there. When he did, he walked over, right past Shelli who stood hidden behind two tourists.

"Can I have a word with you and your friend, miss?"

The surprised tourists scattered so fast from the bench they formed an *I'm-not-with-them* circle on the other side of the casino entrance.

Without turning, the older of the two men reached out and laid a hand on Shelli's arm to keep her from darting away with the others. I guess he had known where she stood all along.

None of the tourists' rides had come yet, but I now sat alone on the bench. The younger, skinny man came over and motioned for Shelli to sit next to me.

I smiled at the crowd hovering near the doors, watching with interest. "What can I do for you, sir?"

"We'd like to talk to you for a moment. That is, if you don't mind accompanying us back inside."

"Not on your life," I said before Shelli could open her mouth. "I came out here to make a call to my aunt. And I am going to—"

Almost on cue, Shelli's phone rang with its programmed song. She flipped it open and from her speaker setting, a tiny replica of Aunt Sis's welcome voice burst from the phone.

"What happened?" Her tiny voice shouted into the air. "I hate these phones. They never work when you want them to."

"Nanie," Shelli said into her phone with enough urgency to make Aunt Sis stop and listen. "We're being hassled here at Western Town Casino by a couple of men."

"You are not being hassled," the older man said almost in a whisper.

Shelli looked at her watch. "It's four-fifteen now. If we don't call you back in ten minutes, dial that phone number Annie gave you and tell Ron Calder, her neighbor, you know, Kaylene's husband, *the Metro cop*," she said a lot louder, "to come in his patrol car and pick us up. If we aren't by the side door, the one you use when you come bowling, tell him we're being held by..."

The man mouthed the word *security* to her.

"If we're not there, tell Ron to look for us in the Security

12

Department." Shelli snapped the phone shut and dropped it back into her pocket.

"I won't take you back to the security offices," the man said, again in hushed tones. "We can talk right here. I just need to know why you were grilling our employees and customers. Once you tell me that you're free to go home—but not back inside our casino. We can't have anyone bothering our customers or our employees. People come to places like this for rest and relaxation—to get away from the cares of their world."

"People come to these places because you lure them here with the false promises of winning riches. *And* your bosses are not satisfied until they've taken everything that customer has."

He opened his mouth to counter my anger. "Now—"

"Don't now me. We're here looking for my mother. She's one of your regulars, and according to the lady we just spoke to, she won a large jackpot in there late last night."

I stared into his cold, doubting eyes.

"So what if your mother came here last night. What happens inside this casino is private. Just go home and talk to her about it. You don't have the right to question our customers or employees about anyone's recreational activities."

"I wasn't questioning them about their gambling." I jumped to my feet. "And I have every right to look for my missing mother!" I shut my eyes and drew in a slow, deep breath.

"As far as we can tell," Shelli said, more composed than me. "After her big win here last night, this casino is the last place anyone saw her."

I locked my stare on his widening eyes. "No one has seen her since that win at midnight last night. So, if you aren't going to let me ask people about her, I'll just call my friend, Tom Farnsworth. I think you recognize the name. He writes the *Out and About Vegas* column for the Review Journal. I can always ask him to write a piece about your privacy issues."

"You know how much of a crusader *he* is," Shelli said peaking around me.

"Why haven't you called in the police?" he asked, his tone softer than before.

"Technically, she has," Ron Calder said standing in full uniform behind the older man. "You know as well as she does that they won't look for her mother until she's been missing for twenty-four hours. I can't even get a warrant to view your security tapes for another twelve. So..." He let his gaze roam between the two security officers. "...isn't there something you can do to help us begin the search for this woman?"

The startled security man sighed with his full attention on me. "Well, with Metro supporting you in your search... I think we can lend some aid—but you'll have to keep it to yourself. I'm sure our Surveillance Chief can allow Metro to look through a few of the security tapes from last night." He faced Ron. "My name is John Kerns. I'm head of security here at Western Town. If you'll follow Stan back inside." He waved his hand in the direction of his skinny companion. "Stan will take care of you until I set things up."

Kerns exchanged a look with Stan and kind of chuckled. "Though it doesn't sound like either of these ladies has a very high opinion of the casino industry."

Two hours later, with my eyes burning from the strain of fast-forwarding through hour after hour of generic security tapes, I stumbled across a glimpse of Mom. I reached out and tugged Ron's sleeve. No doubt he wore that uniform on his day off under Kaylene's strict orders to watch over Shelli and me.

Ron left the TV set where he watched another tape and joined me at my monitor. Shelli leaned over in her seat for a peek, too.

"That's her, alright," Shelli whispered about the woman Ron and I stared at.

"That's your mother, Annie?" John Kerns said from over my shoulder. "No wonder you have such a low opinion of the casino industry. Connie's the worst compulsive we've had as a regular in fifteen years."

"You know her by name?" Ron said.

"We know all the compulsive gamblers by name. Once we're alerted that there may be a problem with a customer, we have an employee make friends with that person."

14

"Let me guess, Elsie?" I said.

He nodded. "That way, we can keep tabs on the guest in case they take to cheating."

"Yeah," Shelli mumbled in my ear while I watched Mom win her jackpot the night before. "They wouldn't want anyone stealing the casino's hard-earned money, would they?"

"Compulsive gambling is a sickness that invades every aspect of a person's life," John said as though he lectured to a group of raw cadets. "And with the depth of Connie's addiction, I would imagine it took hold of her long before she came to this casino."

Shelli rose from her chair. "If places like this..."

I tuned out the small disagreement erupting between John and Shelli and gripped the edge of the desk before me. The woman on screen seemed vaguely familiar, and that hurt. Nowhere in my memory could I find anything that involved Dad, me, or any member of the family bringing that much obvious pleasure to her. It made the woman on the screen almost unrecognizable.

There probably wasn't a day in her life she didn't think of gambling over anything, or anyone. I brushed away a falling tear with the back of my hand but didn't look away from the screen.

John dropped a hand onto my shoulder.

"From the things I've learned over the last eighteen hours," I said to him. "I think I understand her better now and I'm worried that she may be hurt. This isn't California. There she had to drive long distances or set up games in our home to satisfy what I now see as a need in her. But, since we all migrated to Vegas, Mom's been in a gambler's heaven. Lately, if she wasn't at a casino, she was preparing to go to one. I'll bet she counts the minutes until she can take off to gamble. And that's the scariest part about all of this. We have people scouring every casino for her, but so far, she's not in any of them."

Ron reached out to me, but before he could offer me any comfort, John called our attention to the monitor Ron had left earlier. I whirled around to see Mom standing outside the Casino, arguing with someone just outside the frame. Part of a chrome bumper on a car could be seen just inside in the frame as well.

Mom's hands fell to her sides. She stood there stiff and erect,

15

her salt and pepper hair done up in that fifties-sort-of-bob she always wore. Her angry face split into the phony smile she used when trying to win someone over. My heart sank watching her walk toward the edge of the screen until she was gone from view.

A few seconds later, the chrome bumper eased away from the curb, out of the picture, too.

"Well, no one forced her into that car," Ron said.

"Annie, do you think she'd play cards in a private home somewhere in town?" John asked.

"No." I kept my gaze on the screen's footage now showing other people entering and leaving the casino. "She tried to explain her feelings to my Dad yesterday. She said the thrill for her wasn't in winning anymore, but in the adrenaline rush of holding the coins over the slot. She told him her strongest thrill comes from the possibility the coin in her hand — at that moment — is the one that might win." I turned to look up at him. "So, she wouldn't be at someone's home gambling. From what I heard yesterday, there isn't any thrill for her in card games anymore."

"What about the Saturn she drove?" Shelli said, her eyes on the footage of Mom being played again. "Is it still here?"

"Good question." John handed me a piece of paper. "Do you know her license plate?" He stepped away as soon as I finished writing it down and sent Stan to the parking garage. He came back to the desk and sat across from me.

"This is what it looks like to me. After Connie's jackpot, one or more persons, that she may or may not have known, convinced her to leave the property with them in an older car."

"How do you know it's an older car?" I said.

Ron, Shelli, and I waited while John rewound the tape for a third time. "See that?" He pointed to where the film again showed Mom talking near the edge of the screen. "Look at the bumper of the car. Most new models have bumpers that are either black or the same color as the car."

"Good catch!" Ron said nodding his approval. "But this tape also shows the driver has a working knowledge of your casino's security system. Is that the only blind spot you know of in your exterior view?"

16

"No, it's just the largest." The way John sighed and folded his arms it must have been hard for him to admit. "If our mystery driver just happened to park there, it was the luckiest thing they did last night, but did you notice? Whoever drove that car was very careful to stay out of our cameras' view." The grimacing expression he exchanged with Ron didn't help ease my worry. It was like one cop saying to another this-doesn't-look-good. Nothing like squashing what little hope I had by catching something I couldn't unsee.

At Stan's re-entrance into the room we all turned. The way he beckoned John to his side and held a whispered conversation with him, I didn't need to be told what they found.

"Her car *is* in the lot, isn't it?" I said.

John nodded. "Ron, it might be a good idea to get your buddies over at Metro in on this one. I think we've found enough evidence for you to warrant a full search for Connie Capriccio."

17

CHAPTER
3

FINDING MOM

*T*he alarm clock buzzed. I rolled out of bed and crossed the room to open the bedroom door. "Beth, are you up, yet?" My fourteen-year-old daughter's voice echoed down the hall from the kitchen, filled with the anger of last night's argument. "Yes, I am."

Great! I'm still not forgiven. The fury in her eyes yesterday when she stepped off the bus from girl's camp could have melted steel, if that were humanly possible. Yeah, I had no desire to face that at the moment. I went out into the hall and opened the linen closet. "I'm going to take a shower." Closing the closet door with a fresh towel in my hand, I faced her quiet, somber expression.

"I know what you're going to say," I said. "We left you at camp because we didn't have anyone to drive into Utah to pick you up. The Bishop, the camp leaders, and every adult in the family, argued with me to leave you there until we found your grandmother." I lowered my eyes. "Or until the week of camp ended. No one wanted to leave our search to fetch you."

"At the very least, you could have sent a message up there, so I'd know what was going on." She tucked one side of her long, raven hair behind her ear.

I looked into her suffering face. "How could I have done that?"

"Do you know how it felt to have Sister Brandon take me aside before I boarded my bus to tell me Nanie is missing? I couldn't believe you kept that from me. Think about how I felt. I was the last one to know."

"Beth, Kolob Mountain is completely isolated! It would have

19

taken someone driving up there to deliver the message before Brother Riddle brought the bus up to bring everyone home. By the time they did that, they could have brought you back with them."

"Yeah! That's my point!"

The welling tears in her bright blue eyes spilled from the corners and trickled down the sides of her face. I reached out and pulled her into my arms, letting her sob on my shoulder until the extra bedroom's door clicked. I looked up in time to see Dad duck back into the room.

"I need to take my shower," I said, pushing her back and turning away. I didn't want her seeing the tears in my eyes. They weren't out of sorrow but frustration churning inside me. "See what Papa wants for breakfast. We need to get back out and help with the search as soon as possible."

She took off up the hall. I slipped back inside my bedroom, closed the door, and leaned my head against the wood, listening to her knock on Dad's door.

"Papa?" Beth knock again on the door. "Papa? What do you want for breakfast?"

The door opened and I strained to hear him whisper, "Anything will be alright. Don't do anything special for me. I can just make myself a bowl of cereal if you want."

A giggle wafted up the hall. "I don't *think* so. Even if Mom hadn't asked me to make you breakfast, I would have. You know how much I like watching you make faces over my cooking."

I pushed away shaking my head and dropped onto the edge of my bed. How could I tell Beth the things I'd discovered about her grandmother? The embezzling, the kited checks she wrote from three different bank accounts, the endless lies she'd told, all to feed her gambling addiction. How could I burden her with any of this?

Mom had been my daughter's only babysitter since my divorce. They were devoted to each other, their relationship growing into something much closer than even I had with her. Would it be so wrong to let her hold onto the illusions of her perfect Grandmother?

But what if there's more? What else will I need to cushion from my child?

I stood, fighting off the rising panic seizing my chest. The pain almost worse than the moment when I finally decided to escape my abusive marriage. I scrambled toward the bathroom, praying a hot shower would slow the endless "what ifs" plaguing me. Stripping off my clothes, I reached into the shower to lift the lever when someone knocked on the bathroom door.

"Mom. Mom?"

"What is it, Beth?"

"You need to come into the front room. Ron and Kaylene are here. They said they need to see you right away."

I stepped out of the shower stall, whipped a towel around me, and cracked the door open. "Tell them I'm getting into the shower. I'll be ready to go back out in half an hour."

"I did tell them that! They want to see you now. They have two other men with them, and they don't want to talk to Papa until you are there, too."

From somewhere deep in my tight throat my voice squeaked out. "I'll be right out." I shut the door and leaned against it. My racing heart and constricting lungs made it hard to breathe. My trembling knees gave way. I slid down until I sat on the floor hugging them with my free arm. I clutched the towel around me, its soft velour collecting under my whitened knuckles.

If the police had found Mom alive, Ron, and maybe Kaylene, would have rushed over with the news. They would have taken us to the hospital if she were hurt or to the police station if she were in trouble. To come here, and not be willing to speak to Dad without me, told me what they needed to say. I pulled my knees in tight. My vision of the cabinet door a few feet in front of me blurred. Why couldn't I be *somewhere, anywhere else*? No, better yet, I wanted to be *someone* else.

"Father in heaven, give me the strength to comfort Dad. Help me to support his agony when he hears their words."

At the second knock, I jumped to my feet.

"Annie?"

Another set of knocks hit the door before I found my voice

and the strength to answer.

"Annie, are you alright?" Kaylene said. "Answer me!"

"I'll be right out," I whispered with my cheek pressed against the door.

I dressed in the clean clothes I had brought in and ran a quick comb through my hair. I didn't need makeup to hear what they'd come to say.

I opened the door to find Kaylene sitting on the foot of my bed. Next to her stood Shelli and Kathi—the two women I had always loved as sisters instead of cousins. Each stood with their shoulders hunched and a damp tissue in their hand. Kaylene jumped up and gathered me in her arms. The girls joined our embrace.

"I'm so sorry," Kaylene whispered.

I bit my lower lip until it stopped quivering. "They haven't spoken to Dad, yet?"

"No, Uncle Wayne's at the dining room table," Kathi said. "Beth had just finished making his breakfast when everyone showed up."

Kaylene, Shelli, and Kathi went down the hall first, like guards warding-off the inevitable. I couldn't bear to look at the family pictures hanging on the wall between the open bedroom doors. The happy moments they depicted would only make this harder. I kept my gaze on my stocking-covered feet until we reached the end of the hallway where tile from the entryway met carpet. My eyes followed the creamy white squares of ceramic tile into the dining area. Dad sat there eating, slow and quiet. His fork hung in mid-air between deliberate bites of eggs and the piece of toast he clutched in his left hand. He set his toast down and reached for the glass of orange juice next to his plate.

On the other side of the wall, Ron and two men sat on the couch in my living room. Their long faces creating a somber atmosphere in my home.

The men stood when Kaylene and Shelli crossed the tile and stepped onto the living room carpet. I stayed put, leaning on Kathy. When my eyes met with Ron's, his gaze jerked down for an in-depth study of his shiny black shoes.

22

Drawing this out any longer wasn't good for any of us. "Dad," I said. "Will you come into the living room for a minute? Ron and his friends want to talk to both of us."

His eyes filled with questions, but he rose to his feet. In the living room he shook hands with one of the men who introduced himself as Detective Brian Masters.

Everyone found a place to sit. The rocker Dad fell into shifted back and forth, and for the first time since Mom's disappearance, he looked truly defeated.

"Do I know you, Detective?" Dad said squinting at the man.

"No, sir. Well, you know my uncle, Steven Masters. We only met once, briefly. I came to your daughter's wedding with my Uncle Steve. I lived with him while attending UCLA.

"I asked, as a favor to my uncle, that my superiors assign me to this case. Since I'm not personally acquainted with you, or your family, my superiors agreed to let me contact you."

"Steven Masters." Dad's eyes retained their somber look. He turned to me. "He was the last rookie I trained and my partner for two years before I retired from the LAPD." He faced the detective and stretched out his hand. "I'm pleased to meet you, again. Now, when, and where, did you find her?"

Brian sat back, blinking.

"Come on, I worked too many years as a cop not to know what you're here to tell us." Dad glanced at the second, quieter man. "You're from the Coroner's office, aren't you?"

The man looked about the room before offering a hesitant nod.

"Once I realized you weren't just friends of Annie's coming to offer help, I knew. My wife *isn't* in the hospital, or a Coroner representative wouldn't be here."

No one answered, and I stared at Dad. His ever-stoic features solidified into granite, though he couldn't stop the tears from welling in his eyes. I laid my hand on his arm, only to twist around at a gasp behind me.

Beth clutched the outside post of the divider wall separating the two rooms, color draining from her face. Why hadn't I sent her to her room? I had been so focused on Dad I had forgotten

23

she was there. And now, like a kick to the stomach, she'd been told her grandmother wasn't ever coming home.

Her knees gave way and I rushed toward her. The detective reached Beth's other side just as she sagged against me. He gathered up her slight frame, keeping her from collapsing onto the floor.

"Put her on the couch." I sprinted back down the hall, passed Dad's room and entered the front bathroom. I yanked open the door of the cabinet under the sink and pulled out my first aid kit. Ripping off the lid, I rummaged through the box until I found the smelling salts vials. With two vials clutched in my hand, I hurried back into the living room.

Beth lay motionless on the couch, her eyes closed. I snapped one of the vials open and waved it beneath her nose. She stirred and pushed my hand away.

The Detective cocked his head and stared at me. "I dated a nurse a few years ago, and between him and my cousin Shelli over there, they helped me put together a very good first aid kit."

"You mean you're not married anymore?"

"No, I divorced my husband eleven years ago."

A low moan came from Beth and she bolted up, dangling her legs over the side of the couch. "She can't be dead! Tell me Nanie's not dead." Her eyes pleading one by one to the crowd gathered over her. "No..." She lowered her face into her hands and sobbed.

Ron and the detective took Dad aside. I stayed with everyone else to comfort Beth but I couldn't help straining to hear their conversation.

"First of all, let me say that if it were anyone else, I wouldn't be telling the family all of this." He laid a hand on Dad's arm. We found your wife's body in the desert, a few miles from here, out past the new college campus. It's was near a shielded valley that a lot of people use for illegal target practice. The position of the body indicated that she knelt at the time of her death, with her hands tied behind her back. It appears someone tried to shoot her in the back of her head. They missed, hitting her in the back instead. The bullet went past the left side of her spine and into her heart. She died very quickly."

Dad drew back, squinting at Brian. "You're not thinking this is some kind of a hit? That's ridiculous! No one would want to put a contract out on my wife!"

"I understand your doubts, but our investigation is just starting. We can't rule anything out. This shooting puts forth the essence of someone *trying* to make it look like a professional hit."

Dad nodded. His years of analytical, investigative police work overriding his emotions. I shook my head, this wasn't some stranger they were discussing, it was his Wife.

"Calculating in the missing person's case you filed with the forensic evidence we've gathered so far, we have a pretty good idea of the time of death —"

"Stop it!" My nerves couldn't take any more of the cold spewing of facts about her death. "Mom's not just another case, Dad. She is — was your wife. How can you talk like that — like it doesn't hurt to find out she's gone?"

"Annie," Dad said, coming to my side. He wrung his hands together. "I need to find out what they know, to see if they can solve this case. You can grieve now, but I can't. Not until this is over."

Shelli, Kathi, and Beth went through the rest of the morning with moist eyes. I couldn't help wondering where the tears inside me had gone.

The representative of the Coroner's office pulled a packet from his briefcase. He turned its contents out onto the coffee table, and an 8x10 picture skidded across the table and onto the floor at Dad's feet. Dad reached down but pulled his hand back before picking it up.

For the first time in so long that I couldn't remember when, I saw pain on my father's face. I reached down and retrieved the picture, placing it on the table. It showed the items from Mom's wallet, laid out in orderly lines. My high school graduation picture, always in Mom's wallet, stared back at me as well as pictures of Beth from infancy to her recent freshman year. Even Mom's driver's license and social security card were there. My gaze fell on the upper left-hand corner of the photo and I gasped.

25

Next to Mom's wallet lay a wad of Money, fanned out.

That money had to be from the win I'd witnessed on the casino's security tape. I counted the cash shown—twelve one-hundred-dollar bills, two twenties, a five, and six ones.

"Well," I said drawing everyone's attention, "it's clear whoever did this wasn't after her money."

"Yes," Detective Masters said confirming my thought. "We came to that conclusion early on. That's why we need to interview everyone that knew the victim."

"Her name is Connie." Beth lurched over the papers, slamming her hands down on the table. "She isn't anyone's *victim*. She never was! You have to call her Connie. Do you hear me?"

"Beth." Kathi reached out for Beth's arm to pull her back. "He's only doing his job."

"I don't care. I don't want anyone talking about Nanie like that. She's a..." A whimpered sob escaped her lips. "...*was* a strong person. Never a victim!"

Shelli jumped up at the ring of the doorbell. The sight of Aunt Sis and Saunta walking through my door brought far more apprehension than relief.

"What have you found out about my sister's death?" Aunt Sis said standing with her hands on her hips.

"And you know that she is dead, how?" Detective Masters sat up a little taller.

"My granddaughter, Shelli, called me fifteen minutes ago and told me you found Mama-Doll's body in the desert, that's how." She turned away from the detective. In a softer voice, she spoke to Beth and me. "How are you four holding up?"

Beth broke into another set of sobs. I slipped my arm around her shoulder.

"Who is Mama-Doll?" Detective Masters whispered over the top of Beth's head.

"Saunta!" Aunt Sis nudged her cousin toward the couch. "Take Beth to her room and stay with her. Make her lay down until she comes to terms with the situation."

I wasn't in the mood to have her take command of my household. "Aunt Sis, she wants to be here. She needs to know

26

what's happened as much as Dad and I do."

"Annie, it would be better to let the girl get some rest and calm herself. Besides," she said giving me a sidelong look, "we have things to discuss that she doesn't need to hear about, yet."

"*Who* is Mama-Doll?" Detective Masters asked again, louder this time.

I nodded and urged Beth off the couch. Saunta took my daughter by the arm, and they disappeared down the hall. Since Beth's room sat across from mine at the back end of my four-bedroom house, I hoped she would not overhear our conversation, especially with the door closed. Saunta, with strangers in the house, would definitely close that door tight.

I watched Aunt Sis with a careful eye, until she took a seat in the rocking chair. "Okay, what is so secretive that I had to send my daughter to her room?"

"Mama-Doll is your victim's family nickname," Aunt Sis said to the detective, ignoring me. "And my twin brother, Stephano, told me not to let you discuss anything about our sister without him being here." She folded her arms across her chest and stared at us, tight-lipped.

CHAPTER
4

THE NEWS SPREADS

*U*ncle Stephano, "Dolly" as the family called him because of the good looks he had sported all his life, ushered Nana into my house. He let the screen close but held the front door open. Relatives parked cars outside and made their way up my driveway.

Should I rent a hall, or are you going to send some of them home?" I did not want to deal with that many relatives at this moment.

"Kathi," he said, and she rose to her feet, "tell your Aunt Carmen and Uncle Joe, and your Uncle Vince that I said to coordinate things from Ramona's house. If we need them, they can come back here later." He led Nana to the rocking chair Aunt Sis had vacated. "Have them tell the others they can wait outside or they can go home. We'll call when we have something definite to tell them. Have Carmen coordinate a meal to bring in, and make sure the girl is taken care of."

"Her name is Beth, Uncle Dolly," I said.

"We'll use this house as our base because no one wants to work out of that apartment complex," he went on, ignoring me.

"Base for what?" The detective's eyes went wide, but Uncle Dolly ignored him, too.

Uncle Dolly, as Nana's oldest son, held the position of head of the family. He let Aunt Sis think she ran things in what she liked to call her continuation of Nana's matriarchal order. The truth was, Uncle Dolly made the major decisions that affected the family as a whole, that is, after he talked it over with Nana.

Uncle Dolly had good connections in Vegas and those connections worked well. After the parts of the family who had stayed in California followed him here eight years ago, his associates helped us all settle into the community. He even made sure that I, a divorced woman, with very little credit to my name, held enough clout to finance my home at a comfortable rate of interest. I always wondered if he gave the bank some unspoken co-signing agreement. The bank had *bent over backwards*, so to speak, to finance my purchase and even offered me a job.

Crossing the room, Dolly took a seat in the recliner. He sat there, straight-backed and regal, ignoring the shouts of outrage his orders sparked outside. He nodded for me to close the door against the noise filtering in.

"I asked," the detective said, "what base are you—"

Nana placed a hand on the detective. "He's talkin' 'bout the family arrangements. He has no intentions of interferin' with your business."

Dad and Ron stood next to Nana's chair listening to the Coroner's Assistant and Detective Masters relay what they had pieced together about the events of the last seventy-two hours. I had been sent to the kitchen with Aunt Sis, Shelli, and Kathi. Kaylene kept floating in and out of the living room. I had a pretty good idea of what kind of looks she received from Uncle Dolly every time she went in there. Even in these days, older Italian men still thought women belong in the kitchen when important matters were discussed—Nana being the exception.

I stopped peeling apples for Aunt Sis's dessert and watched Kaylene fiddle with the edge of the folded tablecloth sitting across her knees. Raising my hand to my face, I rubbed my forehead. I had stopped trying to hear the conversation in the living room— they kept their voices too low.

Aunt Sis walked toward the table, smiling at us. As always, By the frown on her face, she read my thoughts almost as quick as they came into my head.

"You'll get your chance to tell them what you found during your search," she whispered to Kaylene and me. "Just learn to bide your time."

"Aunt Sis, you've told me to bide my time all my life," I said. "You always keep me from voicing my concerns at family gatherings when I disagree with some of their opinions. I grew up thinking you shielded me from things for my own good — but I don't know anymore. From what I've learned over the last few days, you knew more about Mom's obsessions than anyone else, and you kept the truth of her addictions from everyone. How can you ask me to listen to you now — to take your advice?"

"It wasn't in any way your mother's fault, how she came by that habit." A sadness I'd never seen before from her flooded Aunt Sis's eyes.

"You've always defended Mom, no matter what she did, but you don't have to make excuses for her this time."

"I am not making excuses." She drew herself up to her full five-foot-two inches. "Your mother had no choice in her gambling."

"What? Everyone has control over their urges and habits. That's like saying no drug addict can ever lick their dependence."

"Annie, you never knew your grandfather, because he died shortly after we left Newhall. That was in 1940, just after the birth of your Aunt Jennie. He gave up his cobbler shop to start a vineyard."

"Vineyard? What vineyard?"

"My father's dream, from the minute he stepped off the boat from Sicily, was to grow his own grapes in the soil of his new home. He had always talked about having his own vineyard." She glanced away for a moment. "After he and Ma left New Orleans to settle in California, that desire grew to a passion. And when he won that hundred-acre parcel of prime land in Merced, at one of his weekly poker games, he took his shot. He'd been nursing those stupid cuttings Ma's uncle in Sicily had sent him for months."

She laughed. "He left that profitable cobbler shop to farm those grape branches. You did know that he made saddles and boots for the old cowboy stars, didn't you? They filmed all those silent westerns and early talkies out there in Newhall, and we were there to watch from 1925 until just before the war."

"I —"

31

"No, let me finish. Have you ever wondered why your Nana has those scars that look like long cuts slicing down her earlobes?" She waited for me to nod. I did though I'm sure my expression looked just as confused as Kaylene's did at the moment. "Well, your grandfather lived to gamble, just like your mother. One night— just before we moved to Merced—he found himself between extra funds. He told Ma he wanted the pair of diamond stud earrings he'd given her for their anniversary. She hadn't taken them off for the whole month since she got them. I remember her crying. She begged him to let her keep them. She told him that she was afraid he'd lose them in the game. He flew into a rage, irate that she would try to jinx him like that. That's when he ripped those studs from her ears. That night he won the parcel of land in Merced."

Aunt Sis turned from me, pulled out a chair, and sat down. She looked at her feet through the rectangular glass top of my kitchen table.

"I ran for towels and cold water after he left with those earrings and stayed with my mother until the bleeding stopped. I never thought earlobes could bleed that much." She looked up at me. "So you see, gambling was in your mother's genes. She grew up so much like our father. I warned her for years that her arrogance and self-centered opinion of herself would get her into trouble." She shook her head and I wondered if she regretted her words. "I don't know—maybe she needed it to survive, like we need food for nourishment."

Aunt Sis, the stalwart of the family, broke down. Her head sagged onto her forearm resting on the glass, her soft sobs filling my dining room.

Seeing her cry brought tears spilling from my eyes, too. The ones I couldn't find even when I realized Mom wasn't coming home. I put my arms around my tiny aunt, and for uncounted minutes, let her cry over the loss of her sister.

"Ahem."

I looked up at the soft sound of Detective Masters clearing his throat.

"I hate to break this up, but I need the information they say you have."

Aunt Sis ran to the sink and melted into the embrace of her granddaughters, Kathi and Shelli. I saw the Coroner's Assistant and Kaylene rush to her side, too.

I held my lower lip between my teeth until I could speak without it trembling. "What do you want to know, Detective?"

"Can you tell me your version of what you and Officer Calder discovered at Western Town? What the car looked like that took your mother away that night. And, who I should speak to so I can have the tapes you viewed analyzed."

While my two cousins and a now composed Aunt Sis put the final changes on lunch, I beckoned Kaylene from her chair and we followed the detective into the living room. There, I relayed the information we discovered from Western Town and other casino's we had scoured over the last two days in our trek across Vegas. Ron, Kaylene, and Shelli, who evidently listened better than I did from the kitchen, helped fill in the bits I forgot. Between the four of us, Detective Masters soon held a full, detailed report of our activities in his notebook.

Aunt Sis gave her best shot at trying to feed the slim detective and his companion from the Coroner's office. Their embarrassment at her insistence brought a weak smile to my face. They balked at sitting down and partaking of the usual feast that filled our tables for every occasion—good or bad.

I pulled the Detective and the Coroner aside after they made their apologies. "Detective Masters, I know you two have more important matters to attend to, but I wanted to thank you both." I walked them to the door where they said a hasty goodbye. Before I shut the door I whispered, "Please, keep us informed as to your progress."

After lunch and after many family and friends came in to express their condolences, Uncle Dolly took me aside. "We need to talk—alone."

I followed him into my den, and he shut the door.

"Antonina," He said using my given name, which meant I was in trouble for something. "You know how much I've tried to help you, especially after the fiasco of your marriage, and you joining that... church of yours." He shook his head. "Maybe I sheltered you too much after your divorce, but we all feared for your life when you married that piece of crap. But your mother is gone now, and I no longer have to keep my promise not to ask you about this situation. I want an explanation for your behavior over the last two years."

"I beg your pardon?" I asked in total confusion. "I have no idea what you're talking about. What am I supposed to have done over the last two years that concerns you so?"

"Now don't play dumb with me, young lady. Where do you think your mother raised the funds?" His anger grew with every word. "She was desperate to bailout your short-sighted accounting mistakes." His voice raised to a near shout. "She swore me to secrecy, even from your father." Lowering his voice to a whisper, he said, "She begged me to give her the money to save your home. And after all the strings I pulled for you to buy it so easily."

"And how many times are you supposed to have bailed me out, Uncle Dolly?"

"Are you telling me you don't remember that she came up with the $1,500 you needed to keep your house out of foreclosure—four times in the last two years?"

I ran the math in my head. "That would mean that I hadn't paid my house payment for three month stretches at a time, uh... twice a year."

He nodded.

My head hurt. I rubbed at my temples, hesitating as I pieced together what must have happened. How could my Mom could be that devious?

"Uncle Dolly," I said. I had to show him the reality of Mom's schemes. "I will always be grateful for the help you gave me. You took me and my problems on as if I were one of your own daughters."

"That's what families do for each other. But—"

"No, let me finish. I want you to listen to me... carefully. At no time—and let me repeat that—at *no* time since I purchased this house have I ever fallen behind in my payments. In the eight years I have lived here, I have been late only once, and I was only seven days late then. The reason for that late payment was because my check had fallen behind the desk, and I didn't find it until I moved it to vacuum. Call the bank if you don't believe me."

He stared at me from behind his wrinkled brow.

"Do you think I would jeopardize my job like that? Check it out with the bank." I smiled at his indecision. "Now, let me ask you something. Did you know the extent of Mom's gambling? Did you ever lend her money for anything else?"

"Well, yes. I did help her out several times, financially. But after she lost that last chain of beauty shops in California, the ones in Huntington Beach and Westminster, I told her of my decision not to help her anymore. However, I did show her several places where she could secure other funding if she qualified. But I gave her no more money from then on."

"Are you so sure about that?"

With difficulty, Uncle Dolly rose from the chair behind my desk. "Obviously not, if what you say is correct." He paced the room for a long while. When he turned to me, he took my hands and pulled me out of the chair.

Gathering me into a hug, he whispered, "I owe you my deepest apologies, Annie."

CHAPTER
5

HOLDING TIGHT

*H*e **stood in front** of the dresser but couldn't bring himself to look at his reflection in the mirror that hung before him. Nearly a week had passed, and his chest still tightened with anguish every time his mind's eye saw her body lying in the desert. Of all the other dead bodies he had seen in his career, why did the image of her body affect him like this?

How long could he keep up this façade of normalcy in front of the others? If only he could keep these thoughts confined here in the quiet of his room, but he dwelled on the deed every moment.

He reached out and ran his fingers over the fine wood grain of the antique dresser. The cool touch of its heavily lacquered surface soothed his fingertips. A sigh escaped his lips. If only he could soothe his soul so easily.

Looking up, his gaze followed a long, squiggly black line marring the edge of the mirror just inside its ornate frame. That gap, no more than an eighth-inch gash in the silver backing of the glass, cut its winding course through the reflection of the room behind him. It split the reflection into two halves, neither distorted, but each distinctly separated.

He followed the line up until it disappeared under the top of the frame, then back down again to near the bottom where it started.

Everything, even life itself resembles the flaw in this old mirror. Our actions remain imprinted on the glass of our mind's eye – etched there to haunt us throughout time. And our choices are like that line, dividing the sections of our lives into before and after we come to the decision we take. Each fork presentes in our lives, forcing us into our future.

Right now, he stood on the far side of a fork in his life. Yet, his choice had been the only one that could save his family. Now, there was nothing to do but live with it.

No longer able to put it off, he focused his eyes on his reflection. He studied the face that had become a stranger to him over the last month, searching the creases around his mouth—born since her death. He saw new furrows in his forehead, too. The circles under his eyes drew his attention from his gaunt face. Those circles had deepened. He raised his balled fists and rubbed at the tired sockets. Dropping his hands, he stared at the dampness on his fingers. He stiffened. Where had the moisture come from?

Don't fall apart now. He scolded himself. *My family can never know the price I paid for their well-being.*

His eyes begged to close—to rest—but each time he closed them, he lost his focus. He saw her lying on the desert sand, again.

His body quivered.

He couldn't allow himself to regret the decision. What he had done was the only option. If he hadn't followed through with his obligation to take care of the problem, his family *would* have suffered. Someone had to stop the old woman and her destructive behavior. She couldn't be allowed to pile up that massive debt. He knew—more than most—that not all of those debts were financial.

Against his will, he sucked in a large gulp of air. His lungs rejected the sudden intake with violence, and the cough came. He splattered tiny spots of pink and clear liquid across the mirror. The intensity of the eruption and the pain that came with the explosion from his damaged lungs nearly doubled him over. Holding his hand to his mouth, he opened the top drawer of the dresser. With urgency he rummaged through its contents for the extra handkerchiefs he'd brought with him. He always packed more than one. If he had stayed home he would have plenty to choose from, but that had been out of the question. His emotions wouldn't have held up under that much solitude.

The knock at the door jerked his gaze toward the rapping. This time, taking a slow, measured breath of air into his aching lungs, he stared into the mirror. Maybe if he stayed quiet, whoever knocked would just go *away*.

"Are you alright in there?" a woman's voice said from the other side of the door, worry evident in her tone.

He lowered his hand from his mouth and wiped the spatters of blood from it with the corner of an undershirt he'd pulled from the open drawer. "I'm fine." He lied, to calm her concerns.

He turned over the undershirt, wiping again at the mixture of blood and saliva droplets he'd smeared across the mirror. *How long can I keep up the pretense? Can I hold out until my illness takes me down?*

CHAPTER
6

HELP!

It took two weeks after the funeral for my life to settle down. I looked forward to a relaxing evening after my first day back at work, filled with condolences and sad expressions from my co-workers. Beth had calmed enough to spend the night at her friend's house, but I wasn't alone.

Dad no longer had a place to go back to since the apartment owner had hired a new manager. The owner's son now filled Dad's position as the complex's maintenance man. So, with his belongings transferred into my extra bedroom, it had become his room. When I passed the open door earlier, he lay on the bed staring at a muted TV.

Shelli, her husband, Dane, and I expected no company and planned a quiet evening alone with the movie they brought. They had even talked Aunt Sis into letting her great-grandchildren stay at her house for the night.

I had just finished popping corn in the kitchen and stood drizzling melted butter over it when a knock came at the door.

"I'll see who it is," Dane said, beating Shelli off the couch.

I saw Dad peeking out into the hallway when I cleared the kitchen wall on my way into the living room.

Dane backed up from the open door and a surge of adrenalin shook me at the sight of Detective Masters standing on my front porch. I handed the bowl of popcorn to Shelli. Hoping for news, I rushed toward the open door so fast he took a jump backward off the porch.

"Have you found something important?" Wedging past Dane,

I walked out and grabbed his arm, pulling him into the house.

Dane pulled the door open farther so I could bring the detective in.

"No! I have nothing new. It's been three weeks since your mother died, and I still have only the first few scraps of evidence we found at the scene to go on. I came here tonight to ask Wayne — and all of you — for help." He shrugged his shoulders. " And, just so you know, you're the only ones in your family who will talk to me.

"I thought, because of Wayne's friendship with my Uncle, that he might tell me how to bypass the brick wall I've hit with your mother's family. But," he said looking around the room, "if you're busy, I can come back tomorrow."

"No! No, we were just going to watch a movie. If there's anything we can do, we will." I offered him a seat on the couch.

Dane headed for the hall to fetch Dad. I heard him rap on the closed door. They returned to the living room and the small-talk stopped.

From my seat on the rocker, Dad seemed hesitant to enter the living room. His feet still half on the entry hall tile, he rested his hands on the back of the loveseat. He stared down at the cushions. His voice came out flat and cold.

"Before you tell us how we can help, tell me what evidence you've already put together."

"Well, we still have only that one-inch by nine-inch tire track that was not erased near the scene. We also found a possible print in the sand made by the screening we think the suspect used to erase those tire tracks. It's about a mile further into the desert where we think the killer turned his car around."

"You had all that the day after you discovered my aunt's body," Shelli said.

"Have you found no other evidence?" I asked when his pause turned into silence.

Detective Masters pressed his lips together, cocked his head, and lifted his eyebrows, but offered nothing more to my question.

He turned his attention to Dad, sounding almost apologetic. "I wouldn't tell anyone else this, but since you have a long history in law enforcement, and only because of your friendship with my uncle, I think I can be open with you. We haven't discovered anything concrete enough to build a case on, yet. We only have enough clues to know that someone exerted great effort to erase the evidence at the scene. It'll take a miracle to come up with anything that will let us put a case together. Unless we get a confession from someone, all we'll ever have is a minute amount of circumstantial evidence.

"We've sifted through the dirt out there at the scene and checked with everyone in the area who could have seen or heard anything but have drawn a blank. The way that canyon is laid out, it's a protected area — a perfect place to hide the noise and view of any criminal act. Whoever committed this crime knew exactly what the police would look for, and he covered up the evidence, expertly — the way our expertise might allow us to do."

The detective shifted his weight on the couch. For a long moment Brian did nothing more than shuffle his foot across the pile of my carpet.

"What I need from all of you is advice on how to get something more out of Connie's family members than — she gambled. I just can't break through the wall they've built between the truth of this case and the fantasy they've built to explain it."

I tried but couldn't stop the chuckle from escaping my lips. I shrugged when both Dad and the detective turned to look at me.

"Okay," Shelli said, shaking off Dane's warning hand from her arm. "You've hit the major problem with the Capriccio family. They live in a world of denial. It doesn't matter if or when something dire happens to one of them, they gloss it over with a sugar coating. They push all the dirt and damaging results out of existence — at least for them. We've watched them do it all our lives. Haven't we, Annie?"

I nodded.

The corners of Brian's mouth fell into a discouraged frown. "Well, I need to get around that denial and find out more about Connie's past so I can make sense out of her last days. If I don't get into her head and follow her usual activities, I may not solve this crime." He looked from face to face. "I think we all want to know what happened out there in the desert that night, right?"

"I don't know what you think the family's hiding," Dad said, "but there's nothing I can do to make them tell you anything they don't want to."

Shelli gasped. "Uncle Wayne..."

I shot her a warning look, and she stopped. "Dad, we have to help Detective Masters."

He looked down and shook his head from side to side with deliberate slowness. "You want me to twist all their arms at once—to coerce the members of your mother's family to open up to a stranger, even if he isn't a stranger to me. You three know how they are. Even Dane knows that would never work." He turned to face Dane. "Don't you?"

Dane avoided looking at Shelli. He exchanged a frown with Dad and nodded in reluctant agreement.

Heat blossomed through my cheeks. I couldn't believe what I heard. "You would let someone get away with killing Mom because you don't want to stand up to her family?"

"This has nothing to do with not *wanting* to stand up to them, and you know it. You know they'll resist any kind of intrusion into their fantasy world."

I pointed at the detective. "You've been in his shoes, Dad. You've had difficult cases where you needed difficult answers from the families involved. You haven't got the right to deny the assistance he needs."

Detective Masters rose to his feet. "I ... I, I didn't come here to start an argument between any of you."

Dad backed into the hall. "I have no choice, Annie. There is nothing I can do to help Brian with this." He turned, and with no further apologies, retreated down the hall.

I glared after him, unable to believe his blunt refusal to intercede. Dane and Detective Masters struck up a conversation but I didn't actually hear the words they exchanged. I stared at the hall entrance where Dad had disappeared. It wasn't until Shelli touched my shoulder that I even knew she had stood from her seat on the couch.

"Help me get some drinks from the kitchen," she said.

Once behind the wall dividing the two rooms, Shelli whispered, "What is going on with your dad?"

"I wish I knew. He's tight-lipped with everyone lately."

"Everyone except Uncle Dolly," Shelli said. "They're tighter than I've ever seen them."

That's when it hit me. I grabbed her by the elbow and pulled her to the other side of the dining room. "Shelli, I think I understand. He's avoiding giving any help to the police until he can return the money Mom stole from the apartments. He probably doesn't want anyone in the family talking to any detective until he has it all back in their till."

Shelli smiled. "That must be what he and Uncle Dolly have been so chummy about since the funeral. He's got to be embarrassed because of this detective's relationship to his old partner."

I nodded, and we hurried with the drinks.

"Is there a reason your dad doesn't want to talk to me, Annie?" The detective took a sip of his drink. "Do you think he would rather have another detective assigned to the case?"

"I'm not sure what that was about." *Have I just told him a lie?* "He would probably be the same with anyone assigned to the case. I think he just hasn't had enough time to work through his grief, yet. But if there's anything the rest of us can do to help, we will, Detective Masters."

He smiled at me. His expression glowed with warmth, but I found myself cautious to return that smile.

"Yes," Shelli said with a gleam in her eye that I didn't like the look of. "I think I have an idea that might get you closer to the family, and they may even talk a little freer in front of you."

The smile on Dane's face, sitting next to Shelli, filled me with apprehension.

Over the next two hours, we discussed ways to ease Detective Masters into an upcoming family gathering. He actually came up with an idea that Shelli and Dane jumped at but sounded crazy to me. How could I pretend that we were dating? Yes, I could see how it might help the family let their guard down to give him an honest look at any recent changes in Mom's lifestyle if it didn't seem he was stalking around on official business, but us dating? Could I even pull that kind of acting off?

"Okay," Dane said sitting on the edge of the couch, "Beth's birthday is in three days. We'll arrange for Brian to attend the family get-together as your guest. You and he just need to act as if it's your second or third date."

"It's a good thing neither of us is married anymore," Brian Masters said smiling at me. How could he be so nonchalant about this?

"Before you two play this charade for the family, though," Shelli said, "he'll need to know a few more things about you, your dad, and your mother. He especially needs to understand Auntie's relationship with everyone else, and you are the best one to tell him those things."

"How much background do you need to know?" If we were talking about sharing everything I wasn't sure I could go there, and Brian chuckling at my discomfort wasn't making this any easier.

"Look," Brian said reaching over to touch my arm, "if I don't piece together more than the fact that we found a compulsive gambler dead in the desert, I may never solve this murder. I have to know more about her life, the things she cared about, how she reacted in certain situations. Did she only dabble in gambling? I have to know if there were recent changes in her behavior. I also need as much of her background as possible – to understand why things happened the way they did that night."

"Well, when you put it like that, how could I refuse? Okay. What do you want to know?"

"Not here." Shelli jumped up from the couch. "Let's take this somewhere else? You don't want to upset Uncle Wayne any more than he already is. If he overhears the things you two need to discuss, you know how angry he'll be."

Brian and Dane nodded.

The wisdom of those words alone had me knocking on Dad's door. "I'm going out with the others for a drink."

He didn't look happy about it, but he didn't ask me to stay,

46

either. He didn't say anything.

Coming back into the living room, I found it empty and the front door open. I peeked outside and saw Shelli and Dane pulling away from the curb. Bent inside his blue two-door Saturn, Brian threw something into the back seat. I locked my front door and headed off the porch.

I took my time walking across the lawn, letting him finish his rearranging. I wasn't too eager to answer the questions I thought he might ask, anyway. He backed out of the car and straightened, holding the door open for me. No one had done that for me in a long time.

"Are we meeting Shelli and Dane somewhere?"

"No, they said we should go on without them—that they needed to get home to their children."

I nodded, rehearsing in my mind the long talk I would have with Shelli about me being a grown woman who didn't like being manipulated.

The palpable awkward silence between us while he drove the car didn't help matters. He had only reached the corner of my street when I couldn't take it anymore. "Hey, why don't you turn left? There's a coffee house nearby that way." I didn't drink coffee but the sooner I got out of this vehicle the better.

Once I stood in the crowded shop staring at rows and rows of different coffee variations, I regretted my hasty choice. Sure, they had a few non-coffee items here, and I didn't care if Detective Masters thought me weird for choosing one of them.

"What can I get for you?" the girl behind the counter asked.

"I'll just have a cup of hot chocolate, if you have it?" Brian turn to me and waited.

I blinked, caught off guard by his non-coffee choice. Was this something we had in common or was he just being considerate? *Wait, how could he know I didn't drink coffee?* It's not a topic we had ever discussed. I pushed the mounting questions about this man aside and answered the poor girl still waiting for me to give my order. "Uh...I'll take a medium Caramel Apple Cider, please."

"Anything else?" Brian said.

I shook my head and returned his smile. "Is it too late for

47

coffee?" Maybe that's why he hadn't ordered it.

He never answered and the awkward silence returned until our order arrived.

Looking around, I spotted an empty table in the corner. I pointed in that direction and he nodded.

"You have to excuse Shelli and Dane," I said, a chattiness taking over me. I sat down opposite him. "I apologize for them forcing this private time on us tonight. They think I've been alone too long." I stared down at my cup. "I hope you're not too uncomfortable." *I doubt he's more uncomfortable than I am.*

"I was about to suggest us going alone, myself, so don't be embarrassed. What kind of friends did your mother have?" he said slipping into his professional role. "I mean, did she have a particular type of friend she hung around with?"

I couldn't have been more grateful for being treated like a character witness again. It eased my frazzled nerves. "She only associated with a few people, but they never visited each other's homes, that I know of. She never invited them to family or social events. I've never thought about it before, but I don't think they ever did anything together except hang out at casinos. Dad only spoke of one couple—Dick and Alice—and they didn't even come to Mom's funeral. It's sad. If it hadn't been for our extended family and my friends at church, we might have had only three or four people attend her services." I dropped my gaze again, surprised to see he held a small notebook and pen in hand.

"I saw that." He stopped writing and laid his hand over the notepad in such a way I couldn't read what he'd written. "Can you tell me the names of any of her other friends?"

I considered for a moment telling him I didn't like him being sneaky, but the more I thought about it I realized writing down my testimony was a good idea. I couldn't expect him to memorize everything I said. I took a careful sip of my hot drink and thought hard about it. I shook my head. "I don't know their names. I did see a few of them, but no one ever introduced us."

"Okay then, give me Alice and Dick's last name, and I can find out that way."

"I think their last name is Mesker, but I'm not sure."

"Good, I'll check them out tomorrow. Now, tell me what your mom did for a living. What was she trained to do?"

"The only thing she did over the last eight years was to manage apartments. She always worked as manager and Dad as the head of maintenance for the complexes. Before we all moved here from California, she owned from one to three beauty shops at a time."

"So, you grew up never wanting for anything. I mean..." He grimaced and looked up from the small notebook he wrote in. "... sounds like your family was pretty well off."

I coughed, choking on the hot liquid in my mouth. "My immediate family lived it up in spurts. Well, that's how I saw it anyway. At times, Mom lived as though she had enough money to buy Europe. In elementary school and during junior high, I never had any concerns about money, or about being rich or poor. I had absolutely no idea my mom had any kind of problem, either. I guess, I thought we lived normal, ordinary lives. Most of the time our family had enough food on the table. We had enough clean, presentable clothes to wear. But, there were those times..."

I placed my cup on the table. With one hand I held onto the stiff cardboard skirt around its center, and with the other, I twisted the cup in a slow circle by its lid. I fought back a rising guilt over the tears I still had not shed for Mom.

"I remember years though, when we made no shopping trip for school clothes or supplies." I looked up at him. "Try to imagine being dropped off to visit relatives and being told to stay through dinner. Luckily, my aunts always fed everyone within earshot at dinnertime. Mom told me not to tell anyone when we didn't have food in the house. She told me just to sit there quietly and not to come home until after they fed me.

"Do you know what it's like to move fourteen times in just a matter of a few years?"

He shook his head.

"No, I guess you wouldn't, but I do. We moved that often during my three years of high school," I whispered. "Mostly, they evicted us for not paying the rent, but I remember once during

49

that time she filed bankruptcy, and we had to move anyway. In high school, I added things up once. I figured out that she made good money with those beauty shops. One year — 1975, I think — I snuck a look at her tax returns. She made $85,000 that year. And from what I overheard, that's only the part of her income that she reported to the IRS."

I studied his face for a moment. "You know, I accused her once of not loving me — her only child. I thought she withheld clothing and other essentials out of hatred... or jealousy, as someone suggested. That's when I looked for ways to earn my own money."

I looked across the room, letting my thoughts drift back to that moment.

"I don't have any money, Mom," I said straightening the shirt before me, but never turning from the ironing board.

"I know you're making money with your babysitting and this ironing you do for other people. It's humiliating. Your Aunt Sis told me you've even hired yourself out to clean houses." She gripped my shoulder and spun me around. "How do you think it makes me look to my friends when my daughter has money to buy things and the family hasn't enough to buy a decent meal? It makes me look bad."

"I don't care what your friends think," I whispered, my eyes studying the floor and making sure the hot iron I held out of her reach didn't touch my left knee. "I only wanted to buy a new pair of shoes and some school clothes." I raised my eyes until they nearly met with Mom's. "I need lunch money, too. There's never any leftovers to take to school for lunch."

She ripped the iron from my hand and flung it across the room. "You little — "

I squeezed my eyes shut, wishing I could forget the string of unwarranted, vile names she had called me and the dent the iron had made in the wall. I pushed away the memory of how she later made it my fault when my father saw the damage.

I stopped playing with my cup and looked around the room.

"Since a minor can't have a bank account without the signature of an adult, every time I turned around she had emptied my savings. I learned—very quick—not to keep my money in the bank."

Brian opened his mouth, but no words came out, so I went on. "She knew I made money with the odd jobs I did, because she saw me buying school things and clothes. When she didn't find my money in the bank, or where I had stashed it, her temper went berserk. One time, as a freshman in high school, before I had even started dating, she called me every vile name she could think of because I wouldn't give her my money. I wish I could say her tactics never worked, but there were lots of times when I threw what I had saved at her from the hiding places around my room." I shrugged. "She knew all the right buttons to push."

"That didn't stop when I married and had children, either. Beth loved her more than anyone in the world, but even she knew we could never leave money in plain sight when Mom visited the house."

"I'm sorry to make you relive such bad memories." Brian kept his gaze fixed on his notepad, almost as if he couldn't bring himself to look at me.

"It's okay. I came to terms with my mother's lack of maternal instincts long ago. After my divorce, I took advantage of the counseling offered at a local family abuse center in California—"

"A family abuse center?" His gaze finally snapped to my face again. "You mean, because of your mother?"

"No. That's where I came to the realization that I had grown up in an abusive home. No one hit me while I grew up. Life saved that icing for my marriage. The center helped me see that the verbal abuse from the obsessive domination of my mother during my childhood, set me up. It made me look for the same type of situation in my other relationships. I walked into a physically abusive relationship because it felt normal to me."

My voice dropped to a soft murmur. "If my second daughter hadn't died from that abuse, I'd probably still be there, thinking life was as it should be."

"Was this abuse aimed only at you, or...did your mom and dad

51

fight a lot?" His hesitation surprised me, acting like he wanted to change the subject wasn't very productive for the investigation.

"Mom fought with anyone, especially when she thought she wasn't getting her way. I can only tell you about my experience with her and how it affected me. She and Dad fought all the time because he didn't like the way they lived." I noticed the consequences of my statement in his eyes. "Don't even go in that direction. My father may not have liked the way Mom ran their lives, but he would never hurt her. He loved her. His love for her made up his entire world. She was his purpose for living, so to speak. Why else would he allow her to run their life the way she did?"

We sat silent for a while, but it no longer bothered me. I had given him a lot to process, though I couldn't stay quiet forever. I had a few questions of my own.

"The night we first met, you said you came to my wedding with your uncle. Did we meet then?"

"No, you were very busy with family and pictures and all, but I remember you were a beautiful bride."

"All brides are beautiful on their wedding day."

Brian covered my hand with his. "Not as beautiful as I remember you were."

I eased my hand back and used it with my other to hold onto my cup. This many butterflies hadn't flown around inside my stomach for a long time. I didn't want to read too much into it.

"You know," I told him, looking up into his eyes, "if we can get Uncle Dolly to talk about it, you could get a good deal of information about her business history from him."

His eyebrows shot up.

"I found out recently that he financially backed most of her businesses. I never realized that he set her up again and again after every bankruptcy."

"After every bankruptcy?"

"Did I forget to mention that she filed bankruptcy every seven years?"

He shook his head and wrote in his small notebook.

I looked at my watch when they flashed the lights off and on in the coffee shop. "Wow! It's almost ten o'clock. We'd better go. Dad still worries about me like I'm in high school, even though I've been married, divorced, and have a child of my own. Is there anything else you need to know right now?" I rose from the chair.

"I think I've put you through enough for one night. Let me take you home now. We can discuss your mother's more recent history later."

Outside, we walked in silence—his hand resting in the small of my back. I liked the comfort it gave more than I should have, practicing the start of a fake relationship and all.

CHAPTER
7

THE BIRTHDAY PARTY

Walking through the front door of Uncle Dolly's house, I heard boisterous conversation vibrating out of the back room. Beth giggled at the look of confusion spreading over Brian's face.

"How many people did your uncle invite to Beth's birthday party?" he whispered.

"Just the family." I nudged him, my heart speeding up at the touch. *Had it been so long time that an innocent touch could bring on an intimate response?* I turned away, speaking as fast as I could to cover the blush warming my cheeks. "You said you wanted to meet them socially. Are you chickening out now? Remember, I did warn you how loud these gatherings can get."

"Loud is one thing, but...should I have brought ear plugs?"

Beth scowled. "Not if you want to hear the dirt they throw around about Nanie. It's always been their favorite topic of discussion. I don't think a little thing like her death will stop any of them."

"Beth!" I touched her arm, trying to relax us both. "If you can't handle this yet, maybe we should go home and celebrate your birthday by ourselves—with just Papa."

"No, I know Detective Masters needs to do this. He has to find out all he can about Nanie. But you know how much I hate the way they talk about her at these parties. I don't know how Papa ever stood it. I just wonder how much worse it'll be now that she isn't here to stand up to them."

She turned to face Brian. "Is it true that it's usually a family

55

member that commits the crime in a murder like this? 'Cause, if it is, you'll probably find the person you're looking for right there in that room." She stabbed her finger in the air, pointing down the hall.

"It's true. There are some murders where a family member is normally the prime suspect, but..." He cocked his head and winked at Beth. "...I don't think this is one of them. Rest assured, I've found nothing, yet, to lead me in that direction."

Glad to hear him say that, I pushed Beth in front of us, and she led the way to the back room. The den, what Uncle Dolly called the twelve-hundred-square-foot rumpus room he used for parties, took up most of the first floor of the house. The only other rooms on this floor were a large kitchen, a formal dining room that joined with the den, and three bathrooms. He and Aunt Marisa's living spaces were four bedrooms that took up the entire second floor.

Beth entered the den first and, although hard to believe, the noise rose. Our family broke into choruses of Happy Birthday amid shouted greetings of best wishes. The merriment didn't last long. After one look at Brian and me entering behind Beth, an unexpected, almost eerie silence fell over the room.

I took Brian's hand. The butterflies from my earlier touch still hadn't left but I didn't let go, this was business. I led him through the stillness straight to Nana's side. "I warned you that your presence would spook them," I whispered close to his ear, "but even I hadn't expected this."

I leaned down to kiss Nana on the cheek and noticed Uncle Vince and Uncle Dolly huddled together in the corner behind her.

A hand fell onto Vince's shoulder, and he jumped. "I don't like this," he whispered to Dolly when he turned. "Why is that detective here?"

Dolly, from behind the clenched teeth of his frozen smile, shushed his brother. "I don't know what he's looking for but watch yourself. I don't need you getting drunk and letting your mouth run over tonight."

Vince narrowed his eyes and stared at Dolly. "If anyone ever finds out about our sister's little side job, I'm not the only one who will go to jail this time. I took the fall for you before, but I won't do it again."

Dolly turned his back to the others in the room—the smile gone from his face. "Shut your mouth, Vince." His whisper more like an angry hiss. "No one will be caught. My backers will make sure of that. No one but you knows that it was my idea to use Mama-Doll for those runs, and no one else ever will. Even Elsie can't give us away. She only suspected that our sister was directly connected to the person who sent her to make those exchanges. Elsie and the others all dealt directly with Mama-Doll. Even the men she made those deliveries to don't know who else is involved.

He locked his gaze on Vince. "Addicts always find a way to pay for their addictions, but that doesn't mean that their families are involved.

"Now, go get some food," Dolly whispered. "Make sure you drink soft drinks tonight. Stay away from the booze so you can keep your mouth shut."

Dolly gave Vince a shove toward the dining room. He twisted around so he could watch Annie and Detective Masters begin a conversation with his mother.

"Why have you brought this man here, tonight?" Nana whispered into my ear.

I closed my eyes, hating myself for lying to Nana, and whispered back, "We're dating, Nana. Should I not bring him to my daughter's birthday party?"

A sly grin split her weathered face. She looked up at Brian. "You two come and see me at the house on Tuesday—alone."

I nodded and led Brian over to the pool table, joining Kathi. Picking up two of the cue sticks, I handed one to him.

"Do you play?" Kathi asked him. "It's about the only way you can stay apart from their conversations."

He nodded. "But, isn't that why I'm here?"

We both smiled, and I reached into the nearest pocket for

the first of the fifteen numbered, colored balls. He followed suit, walking around the table at a slow, deliberate pace.

While Kathi racked the balls into the worn wooden triangle, I did my best to ignore the curious stares of my relatives. After a few shots, the conversation around the room grew from a murmur into a low rumble.

I walked behind Brian for my next shot.

"You're putting a crimp in their conversation, you know," Kathi said.

"What do you mean?" Brian's smile showed he took all this in stride.

"Five ball in the corner pocket." I hit the cue ball with the stick. "They don't know what your reasons are for being here." I widened my eyes in mock horror. "They're not sure if it's okay to talk to each other in front of you."

The room hushed just as I drew back to shoot at the six. The abrupt silence captured my focus away from my aim and I missed sinking the six in the side pocket. I turned. Dad stood in the doorway.

Shelli and Dane were not far behind. Shelli's three boys made their way to Nana's side. They kissed her before trotting off to play with their other cousins sitting at smaller tables on the far side of the room. Shelli also bent down to greet her great-grandmother. She flashed me a covert grin over the top of Nana's head before giving her a kiss.

Yes, Shelli and Dane both knew why Brian had come tonight. But they weren't the only ones. It would have been impossible to get this kind of ruse past Dad. He had assured me that he would not give Brian away, and even suggested we arrive at different times.

"Hi, you two," Dad said shouting across the room. "I had hoped to beat you here. I wanted to warn these guys about you dating a cop." After he, too, left Nana's side, he glanced at those sitting and standing around the room. "Have you all lost your tongues? I don't think I've ever heard this family so quiet." He made his way to the pool table and took the cue stick from my hand. "You girls go get some food. I want to talk to this young man."

Dad bent over the table and stared at the colored balls.

"The six is next, but its Brian's turn," I said before following Kathi toward the open door to the dining room. I nudged her at the sight of Shelli making her way to us.

"She's good." I heard Brian say to Dad.

Brian's praise took me by surprise and I leaned on the kitchen's door jamb with a smile. He had no reason to make this kind of small talk, since he and Dad had already discussed our fake dating.

"She ought to be. Your uncle and I taught her how to play the game."

Although it was Brian's turn, Dad banked the six off the side bumper and sunk it in the far corner pocket. Before it fell into the pocket, Dad searched the table for the seven.

Shelli tugged at the sleeve of my blouse, and the three of us headed for the dining room.

An hour or so later, after Uncle Dolly had spoken to Brian away from the others, the conversation in the room approached normal. Uncle Dolly's demeanor let everyone know he accepted Brian's presence — in a way.

With a plate balanced on my knees, I sat between Shelli and Brian, listening to my relatives warming up to the detective. In their clumsy way, they even pestered him for information about his case.

The conversation built for about half an hour before Aunt Jen, the baby of Mom's family, started the usual banter about Mom. I winced at the way she cleared her throat from her folding chair on the other side of the room. The smirk on her face announcing what she couldn't wait to share. She looked, as always, like she might burst if she didn't get to speak her piece soon. Being the baby of the family, she thrived on the fanfare of one-upping her older brothers and sisters.

Her six foot one-and-a-half-inch frame sat tall on her chair. Her height not unusual since most of the women in the family edged up to or stretched just past six feet tall.

Jen brushed her short, unruly black hair off her forehead and fixed her large, intense brown eyes on Brian. "Have you found out about my sister's crooked ways, yet?" She said over the din of conversation.

Shelli grabbed my arm when Aunt Marisa, with her ever-present drink in her hand, stood up. She approached Jen, crossing the now quiet again room. Her chic attire gave Aunt Jen a spindly, plain look. Her jeweled hand clamped down on her sister-in-law's shoulder.

"Jen." Marisa's silky tone cautioned her sister-in-law. "I don't think Dolly would like it if you were disrespectful to the memory of our sister."

Brian leaned over and whispered in my ear. "I don't recognize the accent. Where is your aunt from?"

"California," Kathi whispered from the other side of him. "She got that half accent by growing up with immigrant parents. They fled Yugoslavia just before the fall of the Iron Curtain and settled in Los Angeles."

"Aunt Marisa is the youngest of their ten children," Shelli told him. "She and Uncle Dolly are the *Jones* of our family. You know, the ones everyone tries to keep up with."

"I figured that when I interviewed him at his office over at his swimming pool company," Brian said holding back a snicker. "He has the air of someone who could light his cigars with fifty-dollar bills if he wanted to."

"You need to watch your words." Aunt Marisa patted Aunt Jen's shoulder.

"No!" Jen said, demanding to have her say. "She was a crook." She looked straight at Brian. "When my husband, Jerry, started his trucking company five years ago, he went to my sister for advice. Do you know what she told him?"

"Uh...no," Brian said.

"Mama-Doll helped him set up his business and now he sits in jail. My sister showed him how to set up two sets of books. One set went to the bookkeeper, and the other he kept at home. When the government caught him cheating on his taxes, she turned on that cheesy, toothy grin of hers—*Sorry Wayne*." She nodded to Dad, as if acknowledging her accusations were hurting other people somehow absolved her behavior. "She denied knowing anything about it. Since they found no evidence of my crafty sister's involvement, she got off scot-free, and my husband landed in jail."

Jen folded her arms across her chest. Her defiant stare on Marisa didn't budge until Nana spoke up.

"When you're finished," Nana said, just loud enough to be heard, "we can explain to this young man that your sister had a problem, Jenny. We all shoulda recognized it was worse than we ever thought, 'specially after Annette and Nick came up from Riverside to visit for Thanksgiving last year." She turned to face Brian. "My granddaughter, Annette, always loved Mama-Doll almost as much as she loved her own mother."

Someone called out from the corner of the room. "Only because she didn't have to live with her."

The room erupted with chuckles.

Nana avoided Brian's curious stare and went on speaking, as though she hadn't heard the comment. "We were havin' our holiday dinner at Annie's house last year, and most everyone had gone home. I remember how anxious Annette sounded when she called us there around 8:30 that night. No one but Mama-Doll knew they had come inta town, and they couldn't get her to bring them to the house. Annette cried on the phone, and Nick, her husband, sounded as mad as I ever heard him when they finally got ahold of us. She told us they'd mistakenly ridden t' the casino that morning with you, Wayne, and my daughter, and they had no car to leave in. They begged for a ride t' the house so they could get somethin' to eat.

"So, Steffi," she said, letting her eyes meet with Brian's, "you know her better as Sis, went to get them. The poor dears were starving when they reached the house. They'd lost all the money they brought with them t' the casino early on and couldn't get my daughter to leave her stool even to eat. And she wouldn't let Wayne leave her there alone long enough t' bring them over t' Annie's house."

Nana's words slipped into a whisper. "We shoulda let

ourselves see how bad she got."

Dad rose from his chair and left the room. My normally boisterous family talked in murmurs again. But it didn't take long after he disappeared for them to start up on their favorite subject, again, Mom.

From another corner of the room, Uncle Joe raised his voice for everyone to hear. "Carmen and I learned early on that you didn't loan my sister money, or for that matter, leave cash in plain sight when she came to visit."

"Well?" He shot Aunt Carmen a defensive look when she elbowed him in the side. "You remember when she came over, and the money for Charlene's high school candy sale disappeared, don't you?"

She gave a curt nod.

Validated, he went on. "The very next day Mama-Doll hosted one of them twenty-four-hour poker parties she use'ta have when we lived in Garden Grove." He looked up at Brian. "She had those parties all the time in California."

He sunk into a sullen silence when Aunt Carmen nudged him harder in the ribs. He left his seat but took the plate she handed him before fleeing from the room.

"I agree with you, Ma," Aunt Paul said, turning everyone's head in her direction.

"That's my Aunt Paul," I told Brian. "Her name is actually Paulida. She's like Nana, even-tempered. In all my thirty-two years, I don't think I've ever heard her raise her voice in anger or say something bad about anyone."

Her features, soft like Nana's, wrinkled in alarm. "We should have seen that Mama-Doll had a problem. We ignored so many things that bore it out. I don't think we had a holiday or even a Sunday dinner with you, Ma, where we didn't have to call all the casinos in town until we found her. And, half the time, she told us to go ahead and eat—that she'd be there later. Most of the time, she never showed up." Aunt Paul bowed her head and locked her gaze on the floor.

Brian put his arm behind me, resting it on the back of my chair. His touch brought back that swarm of butterflies. I lost track of things until a commotion in the dining room became louder than the conversation around us. The coughing that erupted from the other room sounded serious. I rose to see if I could help the person in that much distress and everyone within reach handed me their empty plates.

Halfway to the door leading into the dining room, Dad and Uncle Vince came out.

"Are you going to be alright?" Dad said with his hand on Uncle Vince's back.

They walked past me, splitting apart and taking seats on opposite sides of the room. I smiled and went on into the dining room to deposit the stack of paper plates.

"...but you heard what Vince said. She was involved in something like what they sent him to jail for all those years ago," Uncle Joe argued in hushed tones with Uncle Dolly.

I pulled back and leaned against the wall by the door, just a step behind the water cooler.

"Even you could see that she spent more money than she made managing those apartments." Uncle Joe looked over his shoulder but didn't acknowledge my presence. "I asked her about it once—she wouldn't talk to me. And, did you listen to Wayne just now—I don't think even he knew where the extra money came from. If that cop finds out anything about what she got herself into, he'll be wondering what other family members were in on it with her. He just might suspect one of us, and I don't think any of us can stand up under that much scrutiny. Do you think Wayne knows about the things she did for you and Vince? Were you ever able to find out who—"

Uncle Dolly put his hand on Uncle Joe's arm. "Are you here to join our conversation, Annie?"

"No, Uncle Dolly. I just came in to put these plates away. I didn't want to intrude."

I walked over and placed the paper plates into one of the trash cans. If only Brian had helped me bring all this in here. No doubt he would have been a better *fly on the wall* than I had been.

Jo A. Wilkins

CHAPTER
8

DO THE CASINOS HOLD ANSWERS

*B*ells — whistles — the music of slot machines — all the sounds of the casino rang through my head. I hated the way it mingled with the conversation of the gamblers and thundered across the room. With two fingers at my temples, the circular motion eased the noise, but nothing relieved the acrid smoke assaulting my senses.

For the last eleven years, since my baptism, I'd had no connection to this kind of life. Over the last three days, I'd been in and out of Mom's favorite casinos so often I'd lost track of where I stood. I never frequented the casinos. They all looked the same to me. I glanced around to get my bearings. I'd waited here so long that I couldn't remember which casino I stood in this time.

It hit me, the Continental. That's it! I had come here to meet with Alice and Dick.

From where I stood, I noticed one gray-haired, older woman sitting at a slot machine. The way she caressed the poker slot reminded me of the few times I had watched Mom play. The woman, like Mom, never dropped less than five coins at a time into the slot. Her hands flew over the buttons so fast they blurred. She accessed the cards dealt across the screen with amazing speed, her gnarled fingers manipulating those buttons faster than any typist I'd ever known.

She won big for the first few moments. Then, as though I had climbed onto the back of her stool, she turned and stared at me.

"Do you mind?" the old woman said wheezing in anger. "I don't like anyone standing over my shoulder watching me play.

It brings me bad luck. Find another place to stand."

Her resemblance to Mom and her intensity over the slot she played gave me a start. The pit of my stomach dipped and filled with bile that rose into my throat. My mouth dropped open, but I couldn't find the words to excuse my clumsiness. I nodded, steadied myself on the back of another stool and stepped back. Turning from the old lady, I walked toward the end of the rows of slots.

Where are you Alice and Dick? I glanced at my watch—3:15. They were supposed to be here at 3:00.

Stroking the underside of my chin, I heard someone nearby curse the machine he sat before. I swallowed hard against the smoke burning my throat.

Had they stood me up? How much longer would a sane person wait before deciding for sure? But what if they knew more about what I had overheard at Beth's party? They had spent enough time with Mom. I felt sure they would know something more. Although getting anything out of them, even if they did have information, might not be possible.

Over the noise of the room, I recognized Alice's high-pitched voice. I looked up to see them walking up the center aisle, about ten rows of machines from where I stood.

Alice smiled and waved, but Dick, straight-backed and stiff, looked up and down the aisles at the gamblers depositing their coins. *Is he jealous of the gamblers? Does he wish he were there instead of meeting with me?*

Alice gave me a more than polite hug. Her face filled with a big, bright smile, her short gray hair flipped in little curls around her chubby face. Dick towered over both of us. He nodded his thin head in curt recognition of my presence.

"Can I buy you guys something to drink?" I clarified my offer when he smirked down at me. "In the coffee shop?"

He grunted. "That's right. You're a Mormon now."

I gave him a pleasant smile, though my insides churned. I turned, not needing to hear another bashing on my religious beliefs, not when there were more important things to discuss. I led the way to the coffee shop, having deliberately arranged to meet them near it. Once we reached the reservation podium, the hostess seated us immediately.

The waitress came to the edge of the table and turned to me, after taking Alice and Dick's order.

"I'll have a glass of club soda with a twist of lemon, please."

The sour look on Dick's face brought an even stronger sense of dread while waiting for our drinks.

"I really wanted to come to Connie's funeral," Alice said after the waitress left with our order. "How are Wayne and the rest of your family holding up? We were out of town, you know." She snuck a quick look at Dick. "Still are. We've been at my daughter's house in Pahrump. When we read about them finding her body in the desert—" Alice covered her mouth with her hand. "Oh, I'm so sorry to bring it all up, again. It must be so hard for you. But, like I said, we wanted to be at the funeral, only, we were out of town."

"We're having the house sprayed for bugs." Dick's face twitched under an extra forced smile. "That's why we're staying with Alice's kid and her family on the other side of Pahrump. It was just too far to come into Vegas for Connie's services."

Dick raised his fist to his mouth and cleared his throat. Like everyone else in Vegas, he looked as though he fought the dry summer air. After a few tries to clear the clog, he lost the battle and erupted into a cough. Reaching for the glass of water the waitress had placed before him earlier, he took a long, slow gulp. He cleared his throat a few more times.

"Are you alright, Dick?" I said. "That cough doesn't sound good at all. Have you seen a doctor?"

He nodded, continuing to nurse his throat with softer, short mini-coughs into his fist.

"I keep telling him to bring his handkerchief," Alice said directing the statement more to Dick than me, "but he never remembers where he puts them down."

Our wait at the table settled into an uncomfortable silence until the waitress brought our drinks. Alice took a small container of creamer out of a ceramic bowl and emptied the whole thing into her coffee.

While she fought Dick for the sugar, I picked up the straw lying next to my glass. I pushed the slice of lemon down into my club soda and held it there, watching bubbles dance up the side of the glass.

"Ahem." I cleared my throat but kept my eyes down until Mom's friends grew silent. "I..." I struggled to find the right words, even though I'd been the one who asked them here. "...I wanted to speak with you, because I've heard several things about my mom that I think you might know something about." I swallowed hard. "Did you know if my mom was involved in something illegal—something she used to feed her gambling habit?"

Alice sipped at her coffee and never looked anywhere but into her cup. Dick, on the other hand, kept his hands around his hot drink on the table. His locked jaw and narrowed eyes hardened his expression into a cold stare.

Since he was the only one making eye contact, I fixed my gaze on Dick. "I haven't told the detective in charge of her case what I've found. I thought you might feel better talking to me." When they offered nothing, I tried a new approach. "If you do talk to me, I can tell the detective what I've found out without your names coming up."

Alice, raised her head, looking as though she wanted to say something. Dick reached out and grabbed his wife's hand. His expression far from softening.

"Look," he whispered, "we knew your mom did something dirty, but we *are not* involved. Never were! You understand me? *Never*, did we handle any of those numbers."

Pay dirt. I froze, keeping the corners of my mouth from lifting in victory. I didn't trust his denial. "Okay, so you never handled the numbers, but you know what they say about association."

I didn't think it possible but Dick's eyes narrowed even further. "You want to get nasty, we can leave right now. If Alice hadn't insisted we come here to help you out, I'd be at her girl's house in the workshop. No amount of digging is going to suck us into your mom's stupidity. Neither of us had any part in Connie's ploys to raise money to feed her sickness."

Alice, who now looked on the verge of tears, said, "I kept telling your mom she'd get herself into trouble. Running those stolen credit card numbers is probably what got her—"

Both Alice and I flinched at the arm Dick raised. He stopped, halfway to backhanding his wife right there at the table.

My fingers tightened around the fork resting on my napkin. I held it so tight that when I looked down, my knuckles had turned white. There had always been something about this man that I hadn't liked but never identified. Now I had a reason for my distaste of him.

Dick lowered his hand, his lips lifting into something short of a genuine smile. "What are you going to do with that fork?" He let out a hearty chuckle. "After all the years of our marriage, you gonna start looking after my wife's safety?"

I loosened my fingers, allowing the fork to rest back on the napkin but I kept my hand close. "You know why I left my ex-husband. If you're stupid enough to hit your wife here in public, I'll do whatever it takes to defend her."

"Now, are you going to tell me what you know about my mother selling those credit card numbers, so I can be on my way? Or are we going to play games a while longer?"

His smile broadened enough to show both the top and bottom rows of his uneven teeth. "Like I said before, but I guess you didn't understand, Connie didn't sell those numbers. She only took them around, you know, as a runner for someone who had enough access to steal and peddle them. That's all I know, except that she knew the person she carried for, very well. At least, by the way she talked about him."

Dick stood and yanked Alice up by her arm so hard I winced. He pushed her toward the coffee shop entrance and threw a wad of crumpled money down on the table. "I think we'll pay for our own drinks, and there's enough there to cover a tip, too."

Alice just stood there cowering by the cashier's desk.

"My wife won't be talking to you again, so don't ask." Dick stood his ground. "Your mother's death ruined a good thing for her and me. Alice doesn't know a thing about it, and it's going to stay that way..." He leaned in toward me. "...if you know what's

69

good for you."

He joined Alice at the cashier's desk and I slipped my hands over my quivering stomach. They entered the casino and I lost sight of them.

"Excuse me, miss," came a familiar voice from behind me, "is this seat taken?"

I spun around to a Cheshire cat-like grin on Brian Masters' face. "What are you doing here?"

"I had a hunch about you. One more minute, and I would have popped that guy," he said, rising from the booth behind my table and slipping into the chair Alice had just left. He pushed Dick's bills to the middle of the table. "Your attitude changed about halfway through Beth's birthday bash the other night, and I wondered why. I've had a tail on you since about an hour after I dropped you and Beth off after the party. It's just me and two of my friends, and we aren't doing it officially."

"Why are you following me?

"Because I'm not the dumbest detective in Henderson. I knew you must have overheard something at the party you didn't want to share with me but I owe it to both my uncle and your father to do my best to solve this case. So, you need to tell me now what happened at the party. And maybe you should include what you're doing here."

"Do I have a choice?"

"Not really, not with what I just overheard. Can't you understand this investigation will go nowhere if you keep holding things back from me?"

Nothing like piling on guilt to get me to talk. While he ate the food he had ordered before joining me, I tried to explain what I had discovered about Mom's recent activities. "I found out that Mom had a continual habit of using the rent monies she collected at the apartments where they worked to feed her gambling needs. At the last apartments she took, well…"

"Come on, Annie." Brian's fork hung in the air. "I have to know what she did — how she used her time and her money — who she associated with. It's not only for my job. It's also because my uncle called me last night. He gave me a forty-five-minute

70

lecture on how we owed it to your family to solve this crime in an expeditious manner. So, tell me everything, no matter how insignificant you think it is."

I stared into his face, and for the first time, my chest burned with trust. "Dad doesn't want you to know, but my mother took nearly seven thousand dollars from the rent monies this time to gamble on. She took it over a two-week period, just before her death. I also discovered she has done this five other times at three of the complexes they worked for — but never this much cash at one time. She covered herself by moving money around so that it didn't show. That is, at least, until she could replace the funds."

"How could she move that much money around?"

"I've tracked down three checking accounts in her name only. My guess is that she floated checks from one account to another until one of the banks would put a stop to it. Then, she would just add a new account at a new bank. It's called kiting, or, at least, that's what they called it when I worked for a bank in California. I'm pretty sure Dad is working with Uncle Dolly to replace this last money before the new manager finds out it's missing. He doesn't...didn't approve of her actions, but he loved her very much and is determined to protect her name."

"So, along with what I just overheard you discussing with her friends, it sounds like Connie lived like any other junkie. She didn't care how she got her fix, in this case gambling money, as long as it fed her addiction."

Brian sounded sympathetic, but I wasn't stupid enough to fool myself — he was still a cop trying to solve a case. I ended my part of the discussion with what I'd heard at the party. Brian had already overheard Dick about the credit cards so he could fill in the rest on his own.

Anger reddened his face.

"I can see why your father didn't want to tell me about the embezzlement, but he knows how badly withholding evidence can hamper an investigation. With this information, I might have put this case to bed a week ago." Brian stopped to finish the last mouthfuls of his food. He took his time chewing.

71

"By the way," he asked after he swallowed, "what *were* you going to do with that fork?"

"Nothing he wouldn't have deserved." I flashed him my sweetest smile.

CHAPTER 9

SHADOWS IN THE DARK

"**E**lsie," **I said pleading,** "you must know something more. I just talked to Alice and Dick this afternoon, and even he admitted that he was involved."

The casino worker assigned to keep tabs on Mom hid behind her stoic face. She gave no sign of relenting to my questions.

"I need to put this together—to find out who sent her out with those numbers. It's the only way I can find out if they are responsible for killing her."

Her lips parted, but barely moved with the words she whispered. "And if they are—you want to get me killed, too?"

My shoulders sagged. She was right. I couldn't endanger someone else's life. I would have to find the truth elsewhere. "Goodbye." I smiled, turned and walked out of the casino.

The light traffic on Boulder Highway made it easy for me to travel the eleven miles from Western Town to Henderson in no time. Maybe I should have told Brian my intentions, but I had hoped Elsie would be more open to talking to me without him there. Yet, the only thing I had come away with was the knowledge that she knew more about Mom's illegal activities than she wanted to discuss.

I stopped at the red light at College Drive, a few blocks from home and turned the radio down. The oldie, something about a purple people-eating alien with one eye, playing on the station bothered me. I was too tired to put up with its nonsensical lyrics. Yet, laughter began in the pit of my stomach. It came up through my chest until I couldn't control it. I tightened my grip on the wheel, the quaking settling into my shoulders.

I made a right turn when the road cleared, watching through the tears welling in my eyes from the unstoppable laughter. They blurred the road ahead and showed no sign of drying up. They didn't come from the silly attempt at humor from the song. Only a child would laugh at something so juvenile. It had to be exhaustion, maybe even guilt. I still had not shed one genuine tear over Mom's death.

In my weary state, working at keeping the car steady somehow tickled me even more. More laughter, more tears, still I didn't pull over. *I need to be home – sitting on my own couch – with the things that make my world safe and comfortable.*

By the time I turned left onto my street, the laughter subsided. My driveway up ahead made my chest heave a sigh of relief.

Today's search hadn't been completely fruitless, but frustration weighed on my shoulders. Maybe with time and digesting what I'd learned would help me figure out where to search next.

Now that Brian knew everything I'd done, I desired nothing more than to relax. I let the prospect of a good night's sleep wash over me, hoping it would soothe away my fatigue. I pushed the button on the remote stuck to my driver's side visor. The big door chugged its slow ascent up into the rafters of my empty garage. The light inside the cavernous extension of my house flashed on. When I turned the wheel to head up the driveway, it flickered then went out.

Just perfect! I was in no mood to change a light bulb. It could wait until tomorrow. The glow of the streetlight outside would help me see my way around.

Inside the garage, I turned off the engine and lightened my grip on the steering wheel. Savoring the silence, I had no immediate desire to leave the car, letting the darkness ease my tight shoulders. I relished being away from the clamor and bright lights of the casinos. The noise, the crowds, and the smoke, since I hadn't had a cigarette in eleven years, wore on me more each day. The prospect of not doing it any longer seemed like a better idea the longer I sat here.

Maybe meeting Brian out there was a good thing. Why had I

thought I could do this alone anyway? His words rang in my ears, 'You know nothing about detective work and have no business putting yourself in danger.'

I reached for the door handle, pulling until the latch released. My gentle push ensured the door didn't open wide enough to hit the workbench under the window. I swung my feet onto the concrete floor. The summer heat radiated up through the soles of my shoes.

August in Vegas usually gave no one relief from the hundred-and-ten-plus weather until after the nineteenth of the month. About then it always broke and the temperatures would head back down. But tonight, I wished it would all go away—just one more thing wearing on me.

I pushed the car door shut but froze at a scraping sound shattering the quiet of the garage. My eyes searched the darkness, the small hairs on my forearms rippling. The sensation traveled up my arms to my shoulders, meeting at the back of my neck where it sent shivers down through my legs.

I steeled myself against my racing heart and listened. The sound hadn't had time to echo in my ears but it wasn't anything like a stray neighborhood cat crossing the garage floor, the whoosh of the water heater igniting its flame, or the wind whipping an errant piece of paper inside the open door. Familiar sounds wouldn't have raised an alarm in me.

Hit by a lingering smell of a snuffed-out cigarette, I fumbled with the flashlight hanging from my keychain. The pen-sized beam illuminated my lawnmower and other tools. It also fell on the many things my parents had not wanted to put into storage but left shadowy nooks no matter how I held the light.

I had to get out of here. I crept between the car and workbench, saying a silent prayer on my way toward the side door. Could one of those blackened shadows be hiding an intruder?

I laid the back of my hand against my cheek to brush away a stray hair. My fingers came away moist, but it wasn't from the heat.

Was I being ridiculous? Maybe the sound had come from my jittery nerves and I hadn't heard anything at all. There hadn't been any follow up noise after the first one. And as for the smell of smoke—I had hung out in casinos all day—I could very well be smelling myself. I rolled my eyes at my overworked imagination and reached out for the side entrance door.

Beefy hands grabbed me from behind, snaking around my waist. I kicked back at my assailant and screamed, the sound muted by rough thick fingers slapped over my lips. His hands reeked of old, dirty money and tobacco. Opening my mouth as far as I could, I allowed a bit of his flesh to slip between my lips. I clamped my teeth down, biting without mercy. His whispered curses cued me into motion. I let my knees buckle, trying to drop to the floor to break his hold.

The intruder tightened his grip around my waist and pulled me up until only my toes touched the ground.

"I got a message for you." His gravelly voice spoke right behind my ear. "They sent me here to give you some . . . advice."

He loosened his grip across my mouth but did not remove his hand. His other arm remained tight around my waist, holding me against his bulky body. "Are you gonna let me say my piece so I can get going?"

I nodded my head as much as I could under his restraint, fighting against the rising panic inside me. I had to keep a clear head, it might be my only defense. I kept the keys in my hand quiet and worked on popping out the already half-opened pocket knife dangling from its chain.

"You're looking in the wrong place for the person who killed your mother."

My finger stilled on the blade.

"You know about her running those stolen credit card numbers, don't you?"

Nodding again, I mumbled through his fingers, "I just found out for sure today."

"Good! She worked for someone she knew real good. I was told to tell you to look at some of the members of your own family. We saw her a couple of months ago at the Continental, where she handed over an envelope to a man with a strong resemblance to the Capriccio family. If you're smart, you'll let your detective friend know about that.

"It wasn't Connie's gambling debts that caused her death. She always managed to steal enough to pay back my boss. Now, be a good little girl and call off your detective. Stay out of things you have no business in. My boss is tired of you making a nuisance of yourself. Are you gonna cooperate?"

I nodded but my mind reeled with this new information— Mom had also taken money from shady people to feed her addiction.

"Okay then. Stay calm, and don't move until I'm gone. I need to get out of here before your bodyguard realizes you haven't come out of this garage."

His body eased away from mine and I closed my eyes. I never heard him walk away, and I don't know how long I stood there begging my Heavenly Father for help. But until I calmed myself, I couldn't go into the house.

The darkness and the quiet of the garage soaked into me. The man hadn't hurt me, but I couldn't slow my rapid gasps for breath or my racing heart long enough to convince the rest of me.

I stayed there, shivering in the darkness, until a gentler hand touched my shoulder and night closed in around me.

I opened my eyes to a uniformed policeman standing over me. I pushed away the smelling salts he held under my nose, only to notice Beth and Dad standing behind him.

"What happened?" I bolted up until I sat straight against the arm of the couch.

"I entered your garage when I didn't see you go into the house," the officer said. "You were standing facing the side door weaving back and forth. The moment I touched your shoulder you went down."

"Didn't you see him leave?"

"Who, Ma'am?"

"Who are you talking about, Mom?" Beth peeked over the officer's shoulder.

"You didn't see a man leave the garage? He stopped me in there—held me so I couldn't turn around and told me..."

The officer had already turned to leave. He spoke into the small black radio on his shoulder. Before he reached the door, he drew his gun from its holster.

"I have a situation here," the officer said. "I'm at 621 Flower Wood Street. I'm heading out to check the perimeter of the property right now. Inform Detective Masters that we had a breach. I saw no one enter or leave the property from any position in my vantage..." He continued to talk, but his voice faded.

"I told you not to poke your nose into things that don't concern you," Dad said scolding me. "When are you going to learn and stay out of situations that can only bring you harm?"

I looked up at him, tears of anger welling in my eyes. How could he not care about what really happened to Mom? The not knowing was killing me. "I have to know what happened to my mother. I can't just sit back and wait—like what you're doing."

"Go ahead," he said just above a whisper, "look under every rock in Vegas to find out how your mother really lived her life. But take my word for it, you may not like what crawls out from under those rocks any more than I did."

CHAPTER 10

THE WHOLE TRUTH

*B*rian walked in my front door, his face drawn and tight. The smile he usually wore never appeared, and the look that covered his face didn't resemble concern at all. Weird, since he had sounded concerned when he called earlier to say he was coming over, but, now, I saw my mistake. It hadn't been concern at all, just determination.

"Get your father," he said, his tone void of any pleasantries. "I don't have any more time to fool around." He turned his back to me and headed across the room. Taking a seat in the center of my couch, he folded his arms across his chest.

I chanced a quick peek at Brian before knocking on Dad's door. He hadn't moved. "Dad?" I said then waited for the door to open.

The door jerked open and Dad stood there, his robe hastily tied at his waist.

"I guess we aren't through tonight. Brian's here and he looks angry."

"I've been expecting this."

Returning with Dad, the living room turned into a battle-field—the same look shining on both their faces. I'm sure Dad's determination came from a desire to protect Mom and the humiliation of her own actions, but I wondered about this new attitude of Brian's. His whole demeanor had changed since this afternoon.

I turned to leave. I didn't want to hear this particular discussion.

"I would prefer that you stay here, Annie," Brian said, his

tone flat and businesslike. "I know you have more to contribute to this conversation than you think."

"Me?" I spun around wishing I had gotten out of there faster. "I told you everything I know earlier today, at the Continental."

"Just stay," he said. He turned his attention to Dad without ensuring I would do as he asked.

I held onto the edge of the divider, hot streams of anger spiking through me. How dare he order me to do anything? At least from here if an opportunity came for me to ease away from their conversation without being noticed I could take it—whether he liked it or not.

"Wayne, I don't have a lot of patience left. I think you're holding something back that could unlock this case for me. I need all the evidence you've been hiding, and I need it now."

"Evidence?"

"Yes, evidence. With what Annie presented to me this afternoon—about your wife's illegal activities—"

"What illegal activities?" Dad said, rising out of the rocker where he'd taken a seat. "My wife wouldn't do anything illegal."

His performance didn't fool me, and the look on Brian's face said he didn't believe him, either.

Dad dropped back down into the rocker. But, he showed no other sign of giving Brian what he had come for.

"Don't!" Brian rose from the couch, his menacing posture taking a cautious step toward Dad. "I said, I don't have time for this. If I told them at the station what I think you've been holding back, you know what would happen. My superiors would order your arrest for hindering this investigation, and possibly, abetting criminals and their activities. I'm only cutting you slack because of my Uncle Steve. But, either you tell me everything about Connie's involvement in this credit card scheme, and the people she worked for, or we leave for the station right now."

Brian reached under his suit coat and pulled out a pair of silver handcuffs. He let them dangle, clattering in his hands.

I gasped and took a step farther into my living room. Could he really mean to arrest Dad? He wasn't abetting anyone, just trying to protect Mom. How could that be wrong?

"You're not going to take me in," Dad said, shaking his head. "You have no proof that I knew anything about her dealings — shady or not. I, on the other hand, have my daughter as a witness to the fact that I did *not* know what she was up to. Annie heard our last two arguments the day my wife died."

My head snapped around and I stared at Dad.

"If you did have evidence against me, you'd at least have brought a partner with you to help in your arrest. I know your Uncle Steve passed that caution on to you, because I drilled it into him. No matter how well you think you know your suspect, always bring back up in the case of a difficult arrest."

"You're right." Brian relaxed, but only a little. "My superiors may not let me book you tonight, but with the way this all came out, it will cast suspicion on your motives for withholding evidence. When they add the information Annie told me this afternoon, under duress I might add, to the evidence I put together today, my superiors will force me to take a harder look at you as a suspect. And with more than a little curiosity as to why you weren't up front about what your wife had gotten herself into."

Brian moved a little closer to Dad. "All I have to do is tell them about how she ran those stolen credit card numbers and they'll look straight at you. You know they'll suspect your involvement in the whole scheme. You're the one with enough know-how to pull off a scam like that. You are the one who has the background to see the value in selling those stolen numbers. You are the one who knows how the police conduct investigations for both these crimes. They will never expect a sixty-two-year-old woman of being a runner on her own accord. No one will believe she did it without the help of her husband."

"Stop it!" A fighting rush of heat attacked my chest and my face burned. "I won't let you talk to my father like that. Haven't you listened to anything we've told you? We've both tried to make you understand how Mom did whatever she wanted, without regard for anyone else. How she went after what she needed to clear her way for gambling ahead of anything else in her life."

At that moment, I realized I had known all along how Mom

81

had lived her life—what had mattered to her above everything else. The confusion of all I had learned over the past few weeks melted away. I hadn't learned anything new. Her death had brought me out from the denial I'd forced upon myself for all those years.

Brian walked toward me, and I backed up.

"Mom never let anything stop her from doing what she wanted to do," I said with more honesty than I had known lived in me. "And she wanted to gamble more than anything in the world. You think you know so much. Did you or your uncle know that he didn't retire from the police department?" I pointed at Dad. "They forced him out after one of the times Mom filed bankruptcy. The Police Credit Union held the loan on their car, and when they repossessed it, they demanded his resignation. Did you hear me the other day when I told you that she never, in all the years they were married, let him write a check or know the balance of their checking accounts?"

I stopped to catch my breath. I couldn't look at Dad. I didn't have to imagine the horror in his eyes over broadcasting his secrets across the room. Even with his prior relationship with Brian's uncle, this detective remained a stranger. It didn't matter if my breach of propriety horrified Dad, I had to go on.

My voice now a hoarse whisper, like someone else pushed the words from my lips. "I just can't believe you'd think my dad is in any way responsible for Mom running those card numbers. He couldn't even make her stop gambling away all the money they needed to live on. Why do you think they managed apartments? They couldn't afford to pay rent anywhere. Not only did they receive a rent-free apartment, but it also gave Mom a constant reservoir of money to draw on. I realize now why she never wanted them to live with Beth and me. She didn't want Beth seeing the things I hadn't faced growing up."

I sank down onto the loveseat and Brian moved toward me. He stopped a few feet away and turned back to face Dad. "Hasn't this gone far enough? Haven't your wife's actions hurt enough people? Do you plan to protect her until *you, too,* are in your grave?"

Dad rose from the rocker on shaking legs, standing in front of Brian. He straightened his shoulders, composing what little he had left of his dignity. "My wife had her faults, and I learned to live with them. She can no longer hurt this family, but I will not allow anyone to drag her name through the mud for everyone to laugh at. I took a vow forty years ago to protect her, and I took that commitment very seriously. I did my best to live up to my duty while she lived, even to try and protect her from herself. No one has to worry about her problems anymore. So — if you're going to take me to the station, let's go."

He held his hands out, fists down, waiting for Brian to cuff him.

Brian let his arms drop to his sides, the cuffs dangling from his right hand. "Wayne, I've come to care about you and your family." He glanced at me. "I want to... no, I need to solve this case. I need to solve it for everyone's sake. You have to tell me what else — who else — she used to feed her gambling habit."

"I can't tell you what I don't know," Dad said and stalked from the room.

Wayne sat on the bed, staring at the wall. *How can I explain to anyone about my wife? She was always so sure of herself — so self-sufficient. I never had a place in her life, even at the end. Took me this long to face it.* Closing his eyes she stood before him, again, and he relived their last fight.

> "Like I told you yesterday," she said yelling, "I have everything under control."
>
> He marveled over her anger but wondered if he had said things differently, would it have altered the outcome?
>
> "I don't want you to go to jail. I don't want either of us to end up in jail."
>
> "You wuss." She laughed, but no joy shined in her eyes. "You don't know what you're talking about. I'll never get into trouble. I have before and always will replace what money I take to gamble with — before anyone knows it's gone."
>
> "What do you mean you have before?"

"Oh, don't be so dense. You have to know we didn't have the money I spent over the last ten years. You just didn't want to see it. If you weren't such a loser, and could hold down a good-paying job, I wouldn't have to borrow money from the rents I collect."

"I did hold down a good job — until you messed it up." His words, though true, still echoed with the meanness of that verbal jab. She was just so out of control, what else could he have done? He faced her and raised his voice, to make sure she listened. "How are you going to replace three months' worth of cash rents in just ten days? And when you can't, what are you going to tell Hansen when he comes in to audit this property of his? Do you realize you have gambled away seven-thousand-three hundred and seventy-two dollars of someone else's money? Do you even care that it wasn't yours?"

"And your point is? I have enough on Hansen Justeen to throw his butt in jail, too. Haven't you listened to the girls and me talk?" she said, a look of boredom on her face.

"The girls that work under me may have their suspicions about him, but I have the goods. I have enough evidence on his skimming to put him away for a long time. And, it isn't the first time he's been accused of hiding income from the IRS."

He had slammed his fist on the table, facing off with her and that determined look on her face. "I won't let you drag me into this."

"And how are you going to stop me? You have less backbone than anyone I've ever met."

"Fine, then go to the casino without me. I won't go with you anymore." He walked to the phone and picked it up. Had he even dialed the nine before she yanked the receiver from his hand?

"And just what do you think you're doing? You haven't the guts to shame your daughter by turning me in." She pulled in close to his face. "Just think of how your precious little princess will take having her mother and her father in jail. And as for not taking me to the casinos, you'll take me when and where I want you to. And you'll do it with a smile on your face."

Again, he let her place the phone on the receiver.

Wayne fell onto his back and his eyes popped open. No matter how many times he relived that argument, it always came out the same. He sighed. The darkness of the room gathered in around him for another long, sleepless night.

CHAPTER
11

NANA

*T*he knock at the front door came early the next morning. I looked out the peephole, and, after last night's fiasco, a rush of heat filled my chest. Brian stood on the front porch.

We had arranged to meet with Nana this morning, but it surprised me he still intended to go. I woke up this morning thinking he might give up and let Mom's death slip onto the shelf where all unsolved murders lived.

"Hello," he said when I opened the door. "I hope I'm still welcome."

"You still want to talk with Nana, I take it?

"Of course, I still have an investigation to conduct, especially since what I tried last night failed so miserably. I need to step up my efforts. So, you see, I need to have this conversation with your grandmother. I am still welcome here, aren't I?"

Dad hadn't come out of his room yet this morning, but I didn't want him upset by seeing Brian so soon. I nodded and grabbed my purse from the top of the cabinet next to the door. Before I stepped out onto the porch, I called to Beth who stood in the kitchen cooking her breakfast. "I'm going to Aunt Sis's house. When Papa gets up, tell him I'll be back in a little while. I stopped before closing the door. "Make sure he eats something."

Beth put her plate down and leaned against the counter. "He left a while ago, but I'll tell him when he gets back."

Without waiting for a response from Brian, whose eyebrows had merged in the center of his forehead, I shut the door. "I have the feeling you'll always be welcome in my house." Pulling my keys from my purse, I headed for my car.

"I thought we'd drive over together," he said.

"Wouldn't it be better if you followed me to her house? Then, I won't be stranded there if you're called away."

He stopped me by laying a hand on my upper arm. "I cleared the whole morning for this. I logged it as a witness interview. I also plan to use some of this time to—apologize for my behavior last night." He shook his head. "You know, I actually thought I could force Wayne to tell me what he's holding back. But he has a stronger will than I expected. According to my uncle, your father has mellowed a lot since they worked together. I think he thought Wayne had allowed your mom to wear down his strength of will. I found out last night that his values are still there. His strength of character is as strong as ever. It looks like he just buried who he is to keep peace in his family. I guess I have to find another way into his secrets."

I dropped my keys back into my purse and headed for his Saturn. "I don't think my dad's holding back anything more than what I told you about yesterday. I'm sure he never knew about Mom's other activities. Not even her extra bank accounts."

I waved at Brian's friend across the street, who no longer hid his presence guarding my house. Though, after last night, it was hard for me to believe his presence made me any safer.

"How long will I have someone stationed outside my house?"

"A few of my buddies are helping me keep tabs on you, but after last night—" His abrupt stop made me look into his eyes for reassurance. "—Just until I'm sure your family isn't in any danger." He opened the car door. "Remember though, it's not official. They're just friends of mine—we're taking turns watching the house on our off-duty hours. Like I told you yesterday, this case isn't high profile enough to warrant overtime for any of us."

Ten minutes later, we sat on the couch in Aunt Sis's living room, waiting for Nana to join us. I looked up and caught Aunt Sis peeking around the end of her living room wall. She beckoned me to join her in the kitchen with one hard crook of her finger.

I had no more than rounded the corner when she grabbed my

arm and pulled me into her walk-in pantry. "Why did you bring that detective here? You should have better sense than to let him upset my household."

"Nana asked me to bring him over. I guess she has something to say to him."

Not in the mood for a confrontation, I turned to leave but Aunt Sis pulled me back around to face her.

"I want you to make your apologies and go home before your grandmother comes out of her room. I don't like this kind of goings on in my home. All of this is too hard for your grandmother. I don't want her involved in this any longer."

"Aunt Sis, I have no intention of causing Nana any grief. She asked us here. She wants to talk to us. She—"

"She only wants to look over this young man as a prospective husband for you, especially after she found out he goes to your new church."

"I've been a member of the LDS church for more than eleven years. It's not a new thing." Heat filled my cheeks, though I couldn't decide if it was out of anger or embarrassment. Would my family ever stop trying to find me another husband? "And what makes you think he's LDS?"

"Never mind what I know about this man or how I found out. Your grandmother wants to see you remarried before she dies, and at eighty-six, she doesn't feel she has enough time left to let you do it yourself. *That* is why she asked you and this young man here today."

I turned from the pantry door just in time to see Nana making her way into the living room. She wore a floral house dress, her usual apron around her waist. If this truly was the reason for her invitation, she shouldn't be talking with Brian alone. I hurried away from Aunt Sis.

Nana lowered herself into her rocker. "I axed you here today to discuss—"

"Nana!" I said hustling into the living room.

Nana held up her hand. "Just a minute, child."

"But, Nana!"

"I said, in a minute. I want t' say a few things t' this young

89

man. Then, we'll talk." Nana made herself comfortable on the rocker then lifted her left leg onto the footstool. She checked to make sure her arthritic knee lay securely across the center of the stool before going on. She patted the arm of the couch indicating to Brian where she intended him to sit.

I wished for the ground to open up and swallow me whole, but with the determination in her eyes to speak her piece, I had no choice but to take a seat across the room. My head hung in humiliation, but I steeled myself against whatever she might say next.

"Like I said." Nana picked up her crocheting. "I axed ya here t' talk about my daughter's murder so no one could interrupt us."

Had Aunt Sis been wrong and freaked me out over nothing? I snapped my head up and shot a tight-lipped glare over my shoulder at Aunt Sis. She ducked out of sight around the kitchen wall.

"Yes, ma'am," Brian said, sitting on the edge of the couch. The eager look in his eyes matched hers. "That's exactly why I'm here, ma'am."

"Nana, call me Nana. Everyone your age does."

"Okay, Nana. Where do you want to start?"

For nearly an hour, I listened to Nana talk about Mom's life. It surprised me to find out how much she and the rest of Mom's brothers and sisters knew about her habits and obsessions. She relayed stories to him of how they covered up for her over the years. I couldn't help wondering why they had never tried to help her fight her addiction.

Nana laughed with Brian over the arrogance that developed in Mom soon after she learned to talk. They discussed her 'I won't be stopped when I want to do something' approach to life. But the conversation grew serious when they came to more recent events.

"I know my daughter didn't concern herself with honesty in the way she lived her life. How much she could get outa everything was what drove her. I knew she had some kinda secret she kept buried for the last two years. I tried but could never get it outa her. I suspected she got herself inta something dishonest.

"And, the way she treated Wayne was disgraceful. She never 'lowed him to do anything on his own. It's like she tied him to her hip right after he came home from Korea. Over the years, she tightened that rope until she pulled him around like a third leg. He lost the only job he ever cared 'bout—that one with the police department in Los Angeles." She shook her head. "All that happened because'a my daughter's foolishness."

Nana stopped to take a breath and looked over at me. "Child, come over here and sit by us. There's room on the couch next t' this good-looking young man."

The burn in my cheeks returned but I rose and moved to the couch, anyway. I'd given up fighting my family's wishes a long time ago, at least, the ones that didn't conflict with my beliefs. Besides, even against my resolve, something in me wanted to obey this particular request.

"Did Wayne resent the things Connie made him do?" Brian eased one of his own questions into the conversation.

"He resented the hell outa the things Mama-Doll forced him inta. She had a pig-headed, stubborn attitude 'bout life. And I think he regretted marrying her—that is, until Annie came along." She looked up at Brian. "Did ya know that it was his idea t' name this sweet thing sitting next t' ya after me?"

Again, my cheeks burst into flames. I didn't know how much more I could bear of this torture, talking about me like I sat in another room.

"It was my daughter, though, that forced my son-in-law to become a hairdresser."

"Nana," I said wheezing. "Dad doesn't want anyone to know about his beauty license. He'd fall right through the floor if he even thought you told Brian or anyone else about it."

"Nah," Nana said smiling. "He never practiced beauty work. He only got that license so my daughter's last three beauty shops could have his name on the sign. *Connie and Wayne's Beauty Salons*. She had that dumb idea it would bring in more business t' have a man's name on the sign. And, who knows, maybe it did. T' hear her tell it, there were loads of women who called for appointments axing for Wayne t' fix their hair.

91

"But all this small talk ain't what you came t' hear. I been getting lots'a static from my kids. They don't want me tellin' ya anythin'. But I told them it wouldn't matter at all, because ya won't ever solve this murder, ya know. And I want ya t' understand that I won't hold it against ya." Her lips lifted into the same smile she and Mom wore whenever they were up to something. "Ya look real good with my granddaughter."

I had to give her credit, she actually made it sound like she hadn't planned to say it, but I wasn't going to let myself be embarrassed any further. I stood to flee the room but Brian took hold of my hand.

With a gentle tug, he pulled me back down the couch. He remained facing Nana, his voice lowering to a whisper. "I think we look *real* good together, too."

My world blurred on those words. Was this a confession or a ploy? He could be trying to get her to open up to him more but she hadn't really been unwilling to talk. Either way, they needed to get off the subject of me, it was too disconcerting.

Then, I remembered. Nana had told him he wouldn't solve the case. Why? She must want to know who killed her daughter — my mother.

I paid closer attention to Nana and the way she talked to Brian. Her gaze darted to his face more often than I liked.

Who's probing who for information? What is she looking for? Aha! There it is.

Giving in to the sweet, old lady persona, Brian let his guard down and outlined the evidence he had put together to reassure her. She sagged against the chair when he told her about the credit card scheme. But, when he hedged, not willing to name his suspects, she looked like she might shed tears. She even had the audacity to pull a hankie from her pocket.

The way she allowed Brian to stroke hand should have gotten her an acting award. My shrewd old grandmother had learned more about the investigation than anyone else had since it began.

"I really can't tell you who I'm looking at as a suspect," Brian said. "But you can rest assured that if my investigation takes me close to any of your children, you'll be the first one to know."

"We'd better go," I said rising from the couch. "I have a Relief Society meeting tonight that I need to get ready for."

I walked over and kissed Nana on the cheek, ignoring Brian's shocked look, and whispered so only she could hear, "I don't like being used like this."

The innocent look on Nana's face didn't fool me. I straightened and led Brian out of the house.

On the front porch, I stopped. "I'll meet you in the car. I—I forgot my purse."

I made sure he had almost gotten to the curb before I turned and pushed on the front door. It opened without a sound. I tiptoed back into Aunt Sis's house, making my way into the living room where I found Aunt Sis, Uncle Vince, and Nana in deep discussion.

"So, is anyone going to tell *me* what's going on?"

Uncle Vince jumped up from his seat, looking like the proverbial cat after eating forbidden prey.

Aunt Sis clutched at the center of her blouse in surprise.

"Nana? What's going on? Why did you really ask me to bring Brian here?"

Aunt Sis sputtered a few disjointed syllables, but nothing coherent.

Uncle Vince, who sat there staring at Nana, finally said, "I knew this wouldn't work." He looked over at me. "I told you she was too smart to try and fool this way."

"Were you hiding in Nana's bedroom? Or maybe under her bed!" I stared at Uncle Vince.

"I just came in the back door," Uncle Vince said. "I waited in the kitchen until you and your detective left."

"I Don't—"

"Annie," Nana said smiling a sad smile. "We had no other choice. I had t' find out what your young man knows." The expression on her face hardened. "I know my children aren't perfect, and they are strong-willed and stupid sometimes." She glanced at Uncle Vince. "But I cannot let an outsider hurt them."

For the first time in my life, looking at Nana filled my heart with hurt and anger. "You won't let an outsider hurt them? What about how you allow them to hurt themselves? I assume you're protecting Uncle Vince from—maybe that credit card thing Mom got herself into? So, why didn't you ever do anything to help Mom overcome the gambling?"

What I said must have come close to the truth. Aunt Sis covered her face with her hands, nearer to bursting into real tears than I ever remembered seeing from her.

"Tell me, how much of the family is involved in this credit card business?"

"That'll not be discussed here today," Nana said, which might as well have been a decree, her tone falling back on her matriarch demeanor. "All ya need t' know is that your Uncle has assured me that he had nothin' t' do with your mother's death."

"What about the people he works with?" I locked eyes with Uncle Vince. "Can he assure you that they had nothing to do with killing my mother?"

Uncle Vince dropped his gaze to the floor. "No, I can't be sure of anything, anymore."

CHAPTER
12

THE ILLNESS

*T*he doctor looked up in the middle of scribbling notes. He studied the face of the patient sitting on the table before him. Creases around his patient's mouth and eyes had deepened since his last appointment. The patient wore new, darker circles under his eyes, too. And his cough had intensified. He liked this patient—not just for his valor, but because of the texture of his character.

The diagnosis of this man's cancer had come a little more than six months ago. At that time the patient had not reacted like others receiving this kind of news—this possible sentence of death. He only expressed regret for not accomplishing all he had set out to do in his life. Even now the man still remained void of the usual emotions cancer patients displayed. He didn't fight to stay alive but rather sat back, accepting his fate. Not in a morbid way, but with a dignity some of his other patients lacked.

Something had changed in the man since his last visit. He sat on the exam table, calm, as though he had settled his affairs. He acted more at peace with himself than before the doctor had given him the diagnosis.

"I wish you had let us start you on chemo in the first few weeks after you came to me. If we start now, it still may lengthen your life." He held up a hand to keep the patient from interrupting him. "Like I tried to explain, not having the chemo has cut your time left to less than a few more months. If we had started when I first suggested it, you might have stretched that time considerably. And we still could have some...limited success."

"The cancer is spreading rapidly, but I know you have enough strength left to fight this disease. If you do nothing, you may only have another four months." He lowered his head. "Or maybe it's weeks. But if we start an aggressive treatment, you could get a year or so more."

The patient pursed his lips and shook his head. "Like I told you before, I'm not going through all the misery of therapy on top of having cancer. I've resigned myself to dying. I've gone to extraordinary lengths to keep all this from my family." He swept his arm through the air. His outstretched fingers pointed to the equipment around the specialist's office. "I didn't do enough to protect them for a long time, but I have fixed that, now. I can't put them through something like this. It's my time...and I'm ready. I've tied up all my loose ends."

"Like we talked about before, don't you think this is something you should at least discuss with your family? Your wife or the child you spoke of? Someone will need to make your final arrangements."

"Everything is taken care of," the patient said, mumbling something the Doctor didn't catch. "None of my family will have to worry about anything. The hospice I contacted is waiting to take care of me during my last few days. I've opted for cremation, and I want my ashes scattered — I don't care where. Like we discussed a few appointments ago, I want no grave. Or for that matter, no marker over my resting place where my family will muse over the events of my life."

"Have you given the hospice information to my receptionist?" the Doctor said, giving up for the moment. At the patient's nod, he lowered his eyes and stared at his notes. He couldn't bear to look into the man's face any longer. He marveled over this patient's courage, though he thought it misplaced. Every family had the right to know when their loved ones suffered from an illness — especially when facing probable death. A concern he had voiced at almost every exam. So far, nothing he said changed the man's mind. Without consent his family would remain in the dark.

CHAPTER
13

UNEXPECTED CONSEQUENCES

I **didn't have time** to tell Brian what I had walked into in Aunt Sis's living room. When I opened the car door, he was already speaking with someone on his cell phone.

"No, don't send another car. I'll meet them there. I'm through with this interview, and I'll be leaving in just a few minutes."

"See," I said after he ended the conversation, "we should have come in separate cars."

"It's okay." He put the car in drive. "I need to see your father, anyway. Where did he go this morning?"

"I don't know. I do know that he planned to do yard work with me today."

"Good."

I stared out the window on the way back to my house. Only the drone of the car's air conditioner filled the void between us. My focus wasn't on the passing landmarks but how to tell Brian about Uncle Vince, Nana and probably my entire family.

How could I tell him they had plotted to mislead him—to pump him for information? I suspected Uncle Vince of more than a little deception, even with Nana. Thinking back, I realized he had remained unusually quiet about the recent events since Mom's death. During the time we searched for her, and even after her funeral, I hadn't heard his regular energetic participation in any conversation. At the time I chalked it up to worry. Now, mulling it over again, I wondered how much I could believe his denial over not knowing anything about Mom's death.

Just before we turned onto my street, I decided how to tell

him. "Brian, can we not go to my house, yet? I have something I need to tell you."

Brian Smiled. "I wondered if you knew why your grandmother pumped me for information. I figured your silence either meant you didn't know how to tell me, or you found out something you didn't want to pass on when you deliberately left your purse behind." His smile faded. "But we can't go anywhere else. I have to see your father, right now."

"Why?"

"That message from the station—they called about your father. Metro is on their way to arrest him if they aren't there already."

"What?" The words squeaked out from my tight throat. "But they aren't involved in your investigation, are they? What do they want with him?"

"This has nothing to do with—well it could have something to do with it." He pulled up in front of my house behind the Metro squad car blocking my driveway and turned off his motor. He grabbed my arm before I jumped out of the car. "The owner of the apartments where your parents worked has filed criminal embezzlement charges against your father. I need you to not interfere in what's about to happen."

I skidded to a halt entering my living room and listened to a large policeman reading my cuffed father his rights. Following them outside, I watched the officer take the handcuffs off before putting Dad into the back seat of his car.

"As a courtesy, one cop to another, you can ride to the station without them," the officer said. "They'll have to go back on before we enter the jail, though."

Dad nodded.

Beth, flew out of the house, lunging for the officer. I snagged her and kept her back, even though the same urge pulsed through me. Brian had hinted doing so would make this worse for Dad. It was the last thing I wanted to do. Walking toward me, Brian, all business, stopped at the corner of the front walk where we stood.

I stiffened and drew back.

"Here," he said handing me a folded slip of paper. "Contact this investigator in the District Attorney's office. See if he can do anything to help Wayne, or else he'll have a very long stay in Metro's holding tank. He can also help you find an attorney to represent your dad. I don't know if Wayne knew or helped Connie take that money, but from what I heard, the apartment owner is out for blood. He doesn't care if Wayne is guilty or not. He wants someone to blame so his insurance company will pay him back."

It took all my willpower to put the piece of paper into my pocket rather than punch him in the face. This man before me had helped put my father in jail. I hated him—and Mom, too. I closed my eyes. If only I could shut it all out of my head, but emotions I had repressed since high school about Mom's chosen lifestyle roared back to life.

Had she ever cared how her actions affect those around her? Facing the stark question brought a sickening truth that couldn't be denied. My entire life she had never shown anything but a constant desire to satisfy whichever itch she had at any particular moment.

People say it's wrong to curse the dead, but I still cursed her. I had sat through many church lessons on the importance of forgiving everyone, but in that moment, I just couldn't. Like the people at the family abuse counsel I met with after my divorce had described, sometimes rivalries between mothers and daughters never reach a ceasefire.

All the bitterness I thought I had gotten rid of, stemming from her emotional abuse, surged through me. *How could she do this to Dad?* Even from the grave, she managed to let someone else take the blame for her misdeeds.

With my eyes shut I could see her smiling before me, that cheesy grin she used when conning someone gleamed in the sunlight. I heard her voice in my head. "How can I hide my part in this? How can I let him pay for the things I chose to do?"

I opened my eyes just in time to catch Brian's car pulling away from the curb. Turning, I drew Beth into my arms. She sobbed on my shoulder the tears I still couldn't find in myself. For once, I didn't try to push away the emotions boiling inside of me. I let them course through my veins. Mom would not get away with anything this time!

I pushed Beth into the house and rushed to the phone on the wall near the sliding glass door in the dining room. I pulled Brian's note from my pocket but struggled to read the phone number through my unexpected tears. I refused to give up now. The name he had written, Glade Lamoreaux, brought a gasp through my lips. My large Catholic family would never understand my elation, but I knew this name. He was my Bishop! And if Bishop Lamoreaux couldn't help Dad, no one could. My hand shook under a new surge of hope. I dialed the number Brian had written with the name.

"Bishop Lamoreaux," I said my voice trembling so much I hardly recognized it. "It's me, Annie. Annie McBain."

"Yes, Annie," he said. "Of course, I recognized your voice. What's wrong?"

"They've arrested my father." I sobbed, unable to keep it in any longer. I couldn't let it overwhelm me, there was so much more he needed to know. "The Detective assigned to solve Mom's murder gave me your number. I knew you did something in law enforcement, but I didn't know you worked at the District Attorney's office. I'm so sorry to bother you at work, but I couldn't believe it when I saw your name on the paper Detective Masters gave me."

"Did they arrest him for your mother's murder?" he asked.

"No! They arrested him because of something Mom had stolen. For something she did before her murder."

"Detective Masters is good man. He must believe in your father's innocence if he gave you my name. Did you tell him that we know each other?"

"No. I didn't have time to tell him."

"Okay, give me your father's full name and the charges they filed against him, if you know them.

"All I know is that they arrested him for the money Mom took from the apartments they managed."

"Well, since they filed for an arrest warrant, it had to go

through this office. I can look it up on the computer. I'll need to see what he's up against before I can tell you how much I can help. I'll also tell my superiors that I know your family, so they won't assign me to the case. That way, I'll be able to help you as much as I can."

I swallowed hard to bypass another lump forming in my throat. "My father's name is Wayne Easterly. I only know they arrested him because my mother embezzled money from the apartments where they both worked. From what I overheard before she died, he didn't know about this until just before she disappeared."

"How can you be sure?"

"Because, I heard two fights of theirs on the afternoon and evening of the day she went missing. Dad sounded furious, and from what he said in those arguments, he had just found out about her taking the rent monies."

"Annie, I have to ask this. Are you sure he wasn't just acting that way because you were in the room?"

"Yes, I am sure. He didn't even know I was there when they had the first argument. I came through their apartment and stopped before I entered the outer office of the complex. They were already midway through their shouting match. And during their second argument, in my living room that evening, I don't think they remembered they were at my house until it was too late."

"Okay. Now, are you and Beth alright? Do you think you'll need anything before I get back to you?"

His calming voice spread through me like a balm for my emotions. I stopped crying, and for the first time in an hour, composed myself. "I think we'll be fine. I have to call my family... to let them know what's happened, but I won't leave the house until I hear from you."

I put the receiver back on its cradle and looked out into the backyard. My hoe stood leaning against the back fence. The head of it still inside a shallow hole, as though waiting to pull out the next heap of soil. I stared, transfixed by the depression left by its first attempt at scooping the dirt.

101

Dad had intended to fix that broken sprinkler this morning. Why hadn't he gotten further on that little job? He'd gotten up long before me, but Beth said he had left before breakfast.

I dropped my head into my hands. It hurt, and I didn't know how much longer I could hold it up.

Chapter
14

Comfort at its Best

I don't know how long I sat there with my elbows propped on my thighs, my hands cradling my face. At some point Beth joined me. She sat on the floor and placed her head on my knee.

The doorbell rang, chiming several times before either of us stirred. I nudged Beth and she moved aside so I could stand. But, as I made my way across the floor, every heavily laden step became an eternity. My legs, stiff and sluggish, hindered my progress toward the door. I reached out for the divider to steady myself.

The front door opened on its own.

Lawana and Kristen Lamoreaux rushed to my side. They helped me into the living room, and, for the second time in two days, blood rushed from my head. I struggled to fight off the blackness swirling around inside my head.

"Sit down on the couch," Lawana said in a gentle order, steering me by my elbow.

"Thank you. But, why are you here?" I lifted my hands to my face and rubbed the soft skin of my eyelids with my fingertips.

"Glade called me. He told me that your father had a major problem, and we thought you and Beth might at least need someone to talk to."

Beth came in from the dining room and Lawana gave her a hug. "How are you holding up, sweetheart?"

Beth melted into her Sunday school teacher's arms and sobbed. Lawana held onto her quaking shoulders but lifted one hand to swipe at her own tears. Genuine concern for both of us filled her every expression.

Bishop Lamoreaux and his family were the most compassionate people I'd ever met. And it didn't hurt that Beth and Kristen were best friends, either.

"Annie," Lawana whispered over Beth's shoulder, "have you started anything for dinner?"

"No, I haven't even thought about it."

"Okay, you take care of whatever you need to, and don't worry about feeding yourself until we have some kind of breakthrough with your dad's problem."

I nodded but wondered how she would fare against Aunt Sis and my other relatives. They would also want to bring food in to cover my kitchen table. In near delirium, I envisioned large plates of manicotti and fried eggplant, pushing against fried chicken and Jell-o salad topped with, of all things, mayonnaise. Every dish vying for dominance on my dining room table. But I couldn't fight anyone right now. I resigned myself to let them battle it out.

"I have a headache," I heard myself say. I don't know where the words came from. I hadn't felt my mouth move, but my ears recognized my voice. "And someone needs to call Aunt Sis."

Lawana sent Kristen for a glass of water and turned to Beth. "Can you fetch your mother some medication that might help with her headache?" Before she disappeared down the hall, she called out. "Maybe you better make that phone call to your family first."

Beth caught up with Kristen and they both headed into the kitchen. I exchanged a weak smile with Lawana and listened to Beth dial the phone. She tried to explain to Aunt Sis what had happened.

"Annie, do you feel like talking?" Lawana said, her words soft and hushed. She sat down next to me on the couch.

"I don't understand the last two months." It's like the entire world is bent on destroying my family? "It's been one disaster after another." I closed my eyes and dropped my head into my hands.

Once composed, I looked back at my friend, and for the first time since they found Mom, rage burst from me. "How could she do this to him? I wish she stood right here, so I could tell her what an awful person she was."

"It's okay," Lawana said. "It's normal to be angry with someone who's died. And you have to let that anger out, so you can move on in your grief."

"No," I whispered through my clenched teeth, my own voice ringing harsh in my ears. "You don't understand. Her idea of raising me was to fill me with insecurities — on purpose!"

Staring deep into Lawana's eyes, I ignored Beth who came around the divider. "I'd been told so many times when I was young that she hadn't wanted me. I grew up thinking she hated me. At times, I even thought she hated Dad."

I drew a deep gulp of air into my lungs. Tears trickled from the corner of my eyes. I wiped at them in a desperate effort to drive them away. I dropped my gaze to the floor, unable to meet Lawana's eyes any longer. "Mom told me in every way she possibly could that I would never be good enough to be her daughter." *Can I never overcome her words?* "That's what I had thrown in my face, day after day, year after year."

Lawana laid a hand on my arm. "Maybe these are things you'd rather share with the Bishop."

Why wait? I'd gone way beyond caring how others might perceive the messed-up family I belonged to. My tears came steady now, but I didn't bother with them anymore. "I understand now why she suppressed everyone around her — she needed to keep everyone from questioning her actions." I stared again at Lawana through my tears. "If she were here now, I know exactly what she'd do. If they had somehow neglected to arrest her at the same time as Dad, she would have paced the floor, looking for a place to hide. I know she'd be trying to leave town — to get as far away from the mess she created as possible. She wouldn't care what happened to Dad. She never did."

Tears streamed down my cheeks. These truths hit with so much force I buckled under their weight. I gasped for air, unable to stop my thoughts from oozing out of my mouth the moment they flooded into my mind.

"I finally understand what all those family abuse counselors tried to tell me about living with a sick person. They told me nothing I did would ever make my ex-husband or my mother happy. They said abusive personalities must treat everyone else as inferiors to keep others from seeing the abuser for what they really are. They suppress those around them in order to keep their faults and addictions hidden from their own eyes.

"I've tried to talk this over with Dad, but he refused to listen. He didn't want to hear something that would slam his wife." I wrapped my arms tight around myself, fighting off the trembles going through my body. "When he took his marriage vows, he meant every word of them. There were times when I saw how he refused to admit she had problems he couldn't support. Looking back now, I see how well Mom manipulated both of us. She wrapped us up in questioning our own actions so often that neither of us strayed from where she had aimed us."

"Are you sure you want to talk about this with me?" Lawana whispered glancing over her shoulder at the girls. "Shouldn't you wait and talk it over with Glade?"

Ignoring her advice, I wiped at the tears collecting on my chin. "You know, I'm thirty-two, and I only stood up to her twice in my whole life. One of those times came when I married, and we all know how that turned out. She never let me live that disaster down."

"Mom!" Beth said. "Don't talk about Nanie that way. She wasn't that mean! She couldn't be that mean to anyone."

I took the tissue Lawana handed me, wiping away more tears. "Beth, by the time you were old enough to understand things, she didn't hide her gambling anymore. She didn't have to hide anything except how she paid for her addiction."

"No, you're wrong. I knew she gambled more than normal. I'd have to be an idiot not to see that, but I know she loved us. She wouldn't do anything that would hurt us."

Her smile, sad, yet hopeful, wanted me to agree with her. If I did, it would be a lie. But, what did it matter anymore? She was dead. Did I really want to taint my daughter's memory of her beloved Nanie?

"You may be right." I let the lie pass from my lips but couldn't stop myself from exchanging a defeated glance with Lawana.

The phone rang and I jumped to my feet, sprinting into the dining room.

We left Kristen and Beth at home with Aunt Sis on her way over to check on everything, but Lawana refused to let me drive to Glade's office on my own. Somehow, her presence eased my sorrow as we sat in the second floor waiting room of the investigative branch of the Las Vegas District Attorney's office.

Lawana thumbed through a date book she pulled from her purse. She raised her head to say something to me, but the focal point of her gaze didn't stop until she locked onto something just over my head. I turned to find a receptionist standing behind me.

"If you'll come with me," she said, "I'll show the two of you to Mr. Lamoreaux's desk."

Through the maze of partitions, we followed until entering Glade's cubicle. Lawana leaned over to whisper near his ear, "So, this is where you hide all day long?"

He stood and pulled Lawana into a short embrace which made the receptionist's eyebrows shoot up.

"Denice," he said smiling at the young woman, "I don't think you've ever met my wife, Lawana. She doesn't come around here very often."

Denice shook the hand Lawana offered, giving Glade a crooked smile.

After he introduced me to Denice, she headed back to the front of the office and we took the seats Glade offered us.

He turned to his computer. "Just let me print this off and we'll use one of the interview rooms to talk." He keyed commands into the computer then opened his desk drawer and pulled out a thin file. "All set." He rose from his chair. "Come on."

His direction guided us farther into the maze of cubicles. He picked up the page he had sent to the printer, and then looked for an empty, glass-enclosed interview room against the back wall.

Inside the room, the view from the window looked out over

less seedy streets of downtown Las Vegas. The federal courthouse, being the most predominate building in the scene. My thoughts turned to Dad. Did he have any kind of window to look out of in the holding tank?

"Sit down, Annie," Glade said in his usual gentle manner, "we need to go over the information I received just now."

I took a seat in the chair on the other side of the table from him. Except for the glass wall and windows and the dire nature of the meeting, the setup matched his office at church.

He took a deep breath, and after letting it out almost too slowly, he opened the file, spreading the papers it contained in front of him.

"Annie, I don't know your father. And, I want you to understand, that if this were just any other case, I wouldn't be doing anything to help him. I'm only doing what I can because I know and trust you. I know you wouldn't do anything to mislead my investigation. But I must say, I have doubts about your father. The circumstantial evidence is compelling. I can see why they swore out the warrant against him."

Tears again threatened to leak from my eyes. I closed them to keep the flow from oozing out. Lawana laid her hand on my shoulder, and I heard Glade shift his position on the leather chair.

"You know how much I appreciate what you're doing," I said looking up. "And you have to know that I have no one else to turn to."

"Annie, I'm not saying that I'm not going to help him, or that I'm expecting anything in return." He smiled. "Nothing except the truth, that is."

I nodded and stared back down at the table. "You know me. I'll tell you everything. I would never think of holding anything back, especially from you."

"Alright, here's where we stand. It looks like the owner of the apartments went through the books before turning over the office to the new manager he hired to replace your mother. When he found the discrepancies between the deposits and the funds taken in, he looked for the source. Everything pointed to your parents. It pointed to your mother in particular, but everyone assumes that if the wife is involved, the husband has knowledge of the crime.

"The owner contacted the police department and filed charges of embezzlement claiming they had stolen funds exceeding ten thousand dollars from his business. He has since revised that amount up to nearly fourteen thousand."

My head shot up and my mouth dropped open. How could the amount be so much more than what I had heard Dad say? "Glade — Bishop, I listened to my parents fight that last morning before she disappeared, and my father stated very specifically the amount he discovered Mom had taken from the rents."

"How much did he think she had taken?"

"He accused her of stealing over seven thousand. He was adamant about the amount. He accused her more than once of taking over seven thousand. I don't believe he ever would have confronted her without being positive of his facts."

"There's always the possibility the owner has exaggerated the amount taken to cheat his insurance company," Glade said, talking more to himself than to Lawana and me.

He studied the papers before him for a few quiet moments. "I want you to tell me everything about your mother and father's relationship. Then — and only then — will I decide if I can help him."

For the next hour, I rehashed the old memories I had dredged up for Brian at the coffee shop and the recent confrontations between my parents that I had witnessed. When I finished, I glanced at Lawana who had remained unusually quiet while I explained how my family had evolved into the mess I laid out before them. She wore a sad smile on her face amid the tears moistening her own cheeks.

Glade reached over to pat my hand. "I've heard enough. I understand the faith you have in your father's innocence. I'll do what I can to help him, but only because of you."

Chapter
15

Good Results

*E*arly the next morning, Saturday, around 9:00 a.m., a car pulled up in front of the house. Walking across the room, I spread apart the hanging blinds covering my living room window. Brian and Glade climbed out of Glade's car. My dad waited in the back seat. His drawn and tired face kept me from turning and heading for the door. His lack of emotion scared me.

What had he been through overnight?

Brian helped Dad from the car, struggling to stand on his own. He moved with great care and looked older than I ever imagined he could look. He put his left hand on the car and slipped his right hand under his thigh, lifting underneath his leg until his foot cleared the curb.

Placing a hand on Dad's back to steady him, Brian shut the backseat door and helped him onto the sidewalk. Glade came around the car to join them, and all three headed over the lawn for the front door.

"What are you staring at?" Beth sat curled up on the loveseat reading her weekend homework. She peered at me over the top of her English book.

"I'm just watching Detective Masters and Bishop Lamoreaux help your grandfather to the door."

Beth gasped and bolted for the front door. I wasn't far behind. She hadn't opened the screen door so I knew they couldn't see us yet. But, Dad's limping struggle across the lawn drew tears to my eyes. I wiped at the infernal things.

Maybe, if I stopped drinking water, the never-ending tears

would stop. I couldn't believe how weepy I'd become lately — a very out-of-character condition for me. I composed myself and pushed on the screen door. Dad entered first. He walked past me and he ran his hand over the length of my forearm. His eyes met mine, and a feeble attempt at a smile crossed his face. I wanted to throw myself at him in a relieved embrace, but, by the sore and tired way he moved, it looked like that would have tipped him over.

Beth, on the other hand, grabbed him, and with Brian's help, guided him to the couch. They lifted his legs, and with their help, he positioned them across the cushions. I put pillows behind his back, and he rested against its high arm.

Beth and I could do no more than just stand there, staring at the exhausted figure lying on the couch.

My vibrant, energetic father, who always found a way to conquer any unwanted situation, lay there, totally defeated. He didn't move, almost as if resigned to letting someone, anyone, help him with everything.

I turned to Glade and Brian, and though I wasn't the kind of person who gave out hugs and affection easily, I clutched my Bishop in a short embrace. "Thank you." I choked on my words when we parted. "It doesn't...cover my...gratitude." I glanced at Brian, adding, "And to you, too." I offered them a seat with a sweep of my hand and they both complied.

I turned to Glade. "Can you tell me what happened after I left your office?"

"Sure. I did a little more legwork and spoke with the arraignment judge late yesterday afternoon," Glade said. "Luckily, it happened to be a judge that I know quite well." He glanced at Dad on the couch.

"Otherwise, Wayne might still be in that holding tank," Brian said.

Glade nodded. "But, after the judge reviewed the circumstances of the case, and after my vouching for your father, he was willing to waive bail and release him on his own recognizance. I gave my personal guarantee that he would be there on his court date in two weeks."

112

"So, this still isn't over?" I fell into my rocking chair.

"No, but with Wayne's law enforcement background and the lack of mitigating evidence tying him to the embezzlement, everything went smoothly. I think the judge saw right off that your mother had sole involvement. And the fact that I vouched for the integrity of the family helped. He saw no reason to hold Wayne over until the arraignment, and he set the date for the evidentiary hearing exactly two weeks from yesterday."

"How do we get ready for that?" I asked.

"Well..." He reached into his pocket for a business card. "... he'll need a good lawyer. I have a few names jotted down." He handed me the card. "Call any one of them. They're all good — and reliable. You only need to find out who can be ready in time for the court date. Tell whoever you get that I will supply him or her with a copy of the case file to get started."

Glade rose from the chair. "Let him rest. He's been through a lot in the last eighteen hours. When I got to the jail this morning with his release papers, he was trying to sleep in the corner of the holding cell — on the concrete floor. I met Brian outside the cell. He'd been there most of the night, watching out for Wayne."

I followed my Bishop to the door. "I have to go," he said. "I'll call you later."

After Bishop closed the door, I turned to Brian. "What *did* he go through last night?"

"It was a bad night. The younger, tougher elements in the tank had staked out all the benches.

"It's funny, but it looked like one really rough inmate kind of took to watching over him. You know, keeping the others from harassing him. When we got him into Glade's car, he told me the arresting officer had advised him to keep quiet about his police background while they kept him in the holding tank. I guess the inmate watching over him looked at your father as just another old man in some kind of trouble."

I glanced at Dad. He no longer looked younger than his age of sixty-one. Right now, he could have passed for seventy-one.

"Thank you, again." I peeled my gaze away from Dad and glanced at Brian. "Would you like to stay for dinner?" His nod, even though I really did want him to stay, brought a sigh past my lips. Feeding him seemed like such a cheap way to thank him. "You know, I'll never be able to repay either of you for what you've done."

"Annie," Brian said, scolding me, "there's no debt you need to repay. Both Glade and I were glad to help."

It took a great deal of effort to smile, but I gave him the best one I could. Turning back to Dad, Beth in the background put her finger to her lips. He had fallen asleep on the couch. His soft snores filling the now quiet room.

The next few weeks kept us so busy I didn't worry about not hearing from Brian. I didn't have time to wonder about the murder investigation. I concentrated on Dad and helping him out from under the charges against him.

The first attorney we spoke to, Mr. Carlson, turned out to be between cases, so we hired him right off. At our first meeting, he went over the papers I passed on from Glade. He did a quick search on the reputation of Mom and Dad's boss, Mr. Justeen, and discovered through a friend at the IRS that they had investigated him twice before for misrepresenting his income but never taken him to court due to lack of evidence. Mr. Carlson speculated that Justeen had a good relationship with a very creative accountant.

At Dad's preliminary hearing, our entourage filled half the seats on the defendant's side of the courtroom. Dad joined his attorney at the long table facing the judge's bench. I sat directly behind him between Shelli and Lawana, on the other side of the short railing that separated the gallery of spectators from those involved in the trial. The members of our family and friends that showed up to support Dad took up six rows. Beth and Kristen sat in the second row beside Uncle Vince, who never stopped fidgeting.

Before long, the representative of the District Attorney's Office entered and hovered near the other long table in front of the railing. He shifted papers around, but every once in a while, glanced at the door in the rear of the courtroom. Maybe he, too, watched for Mr. Justeen's arrival.

Mr. Carlson rose from his chair and bent over to whisper something to Dad. He took his time walking to meet the D.A. in the middle of the room, between the tables. They carried on a hushed conversation over an open file. While they spoke, the D.A. kept glancing at the door. Snapping the file shut, he shrugged. They shook hands and walked away from each other.

"Will the court please rise," the bailiff said from the corner of the room.

The judge entered and I tried my best to prepare my brain for all the legalese that was about to happen.

"Are we ready to proceed, gentlemen?" the judge said.

The D.A. stood behind his table but stopped to shuffle through his papers. "Your Honor, it seems that Mr. Justeen, the owner of the apartments, has changed his mind on prosecuting Mr. Easterly. It seems that he has changed his mind on the guilt of the defendant and now sees that the blame for the crime rests solely on the shoulders of his wife, Conchetta Easterly."

I listened to the legal banter that followed. Questions and directives flew back and forth disguised in legal wrangling I didn't understand, until I heard Mr. Carlson agree with the court that the charges against Dad should be dropped for lack of evidence.

The judge hit his gavel on the small round disk on his bench. Everyone stood again and he left the room. I reached over the railing and tapped Mr. Carlson on the shoulder.

"What just happened? Did they postpone the trial 'til they could bring Mr. Justeen into court?"

"No," he said, pushing his chair back but not standing up. "They dismissed the charges against Wayne, with prejudice." He shuffled through the papers he had laid out on the table, stacking them into neat piles.

It took me a moment to find my voice. "What do you mean, with prejudice? Are they going to bring him back into court again?"

"No. In essence, they have dropped all charges against him."

"You mean, that after all the commotion over the last two weeks, and all the evidence you gathered to present here, today,

115

they just dropped the charges? Why — how could they do that?"

Mr. Carlson finished putting his papers back into his briefcase and stood. He turned to face me. "Justeen didn't show up to testify. And, since he informed the D.A.'s office of the embezzlement *and* was the sole accuser of your parents, he is their primary witness against Wayne. Without him, they have no evidence.

"Evidently, he told the D.A. that, after a further review of the books and extensive questioning of other employees, he came to the conclusion that only your mother pulled off this theft of his funds.

"He didn't show up to testify against your father, and because he was not subpoenaed, they suggested the case be dismissed." He leaned over and whispered, "I think he refused to testify."

"He did?"

Mr. Carlson continued in his whisper close to my ear. "I may be wrong, but my conversation with his personal lawyer of two days may have triggered this. I let him know that we had witnesses willing to testify as to how much he inflated the amount embezzled, allowing him to collect an extravagant insurance repayment. It may have aided in his conclusion that only your mother took his money."

Mr. Carlson's smile put me at ease. "This means that my father isn't going to pay for Mom's crime?"

He nodded and turned to shake Dad's hand. They exchanged a few brief, quiet words before the attorney left the table.

We didn't stay in the courtroom very long after that, either. Beth reached the double doors first and turned back to me with a sly grin on her face.

"Mom, you have company."

Holding onto Dad's arm, I went through the doors to find Brian standing there. He reached out to shake Dad's hand in congratulations, and for the first time in two weeks, I wondered why he hadn't called with news about the investigation.

CHAPTER
16

BE CAREFUL
WHAT QUESTIONS YOU ASK

*T*hat night brought a party at Uncle Dolly's house — the first real party since Mom's murder. Everyone showed up. The celebration filled his huge room with bodies. Once I found a chair to sit on, I didn't let it go. Between Beth, Shelli, Brian, Dane, and me, we kept three chairs secured for the five of us to trade out on. Brian and Dane took the fewest turns, sitting only to save a vacated seat when one of us left our cozy corner.

My first look at the table told me Aunt Sis had put together a menu geared to celebrate both a not-guilty or guilty verdict. No one had expected this outcome. The table laid at the far end of the room held everything in the way of comfort food, with dishes added at the last minute to make this a true celebration.

I recognized that extra effort when I took my first bite of one of her homemade cannoli. It may be Nana's recipe, but no one made them as good as Aunt Sis — filled with a smooth, sweet ricotta and powdered sugar filling, some laced with mini chocolate chips others with citron fruit rind. My favorite — mini chocolate chips — oozed out of the shell when I crunched it between my teeth. The flaky pastry hadn't sat filled long enough for the shell to soften under its moisture. She had even dipped the ends in crushed pistachios and drizzled chocolate over the powdered sugar dusted on top of the shell. A very special topping saved for momentous occasions, like weddings.

For the first time in a month, I saw Uncle Dolly and Uncle

Vince smiling at everyone, including each other. Uncle Vince still shied away from Brian, but all went well for the evening.

Nana smiled the entire time, too, relaxing in her comfort zone. Her family, with only the one exception, huddled at her side. She even looked comfortable with the few strangers in the crowd, enjoying everyone's company.

Dad sat by himself in a special corner of the rumpus room not talking much to anyone, but in the seat of honor, anyway. Every few minutes, someone stopped and either shook his hand or slapped him on the back. His smiles came in short bursts.

He acted as if he expected someone else to enter the room and join the party. That's when it hit me — he waited to share this moment of triumph with Mom!

Since that first day when they came to the house and told us of her death, Dad had held in all his emotions. Now, I watched him sit there, lost in the crowd of her family, friends, and well-wishers. *Does he still think it too soon to delve into the grief he set aside?*

I kept an eye on him through the night. Even though he seemed happy at sparse moments, he stayed at the edge of the celebration. No one allowed him to forget, though, that they had thrown this party for him.

On the way to the buffet table for seconds on some of the dishes I don't see at most parties, Shelli touched my arm.

"Is Uncle Wayne cold? He hasn't taken his sweater off all night."

I looked again at Dad with even more scrutiny. Yeah, the sweater was weird, but his whole life had been turned upside down. "He's been through a lot in the last couple of months. It's probably just nerves making him feel cold."

Her right eyebrow rose. "You could be right. Maybe that could account for his loss of weight, too. But, have you taken a good look at his face lately?"

I studied Dad's face full on. Seeing him every day now, I must admit, I hadn't noticed the drop in weight. But his skinnier frame blared at me now. His sweater drooped around his shoulders and hung well past his waist.

Shelli pulled in next to my ear. "What worries me is how deep those creases in his face have become. I've got patients on my floor that are really sick. I see that kind of effect in them. They lose so much weight that the normal creasing in their face takes on a look like someone carved them with a pallet knife, making deep gashes where normal wrinkles should be. And look at how his cheeks sag at his jaw line, and those dark circles under his eyes. Not to mention how pale he is lately. I'm not sure that can all be from the stress of the last few months."

"He looks so detached." Brian nudged Shelli with his elbow. "He's especially detached for celebrating his win in court."

The concern on both their faces only ramped up my concern over this new recognition of Dad. "I'll keep a closer eye on him. I'll talk to him when we get home."

The rest of the evening went well, I guess. But Dane, once we clued him in, Shelli, Brian, and I continued to watch Dad.

About an hour later, just after a set of twin cousins performed their usual song and dance routine for the gathering, a commotion broke out at the other side of the room. Shelli and I followed the crowd over to see what happened. Uncle Vince sat in a chair doubled over in a coughing spasm that hurt just listening to it.

Shelli pushed her way to the front of the crowd. "Okay, back up and give him some room." She took over in her best nurse demeanor. "Annie, go get him a glass of water."

I ran to the kitchen. His horrible coughing followed me even as I passed through the dining room and around the buffet table, making me cringe. In the kitchen, I picked up a clean glass and filled it from the water dispenser and headed back into the main room.

"How long have you had this cough?" Shelli said to Uncle Vince.

He took the glass from me and sipped at it under Shelli's instructions before answering. "I was at the doctor's just yesterday. He told me it's a...a sinus infection."

"But, you've had that cough for a long time," Shelli said. "Is he sure that's all it is? What tests did he run?"

"He told me the cough will hang on for a while, even after

119

the infection is gone." Uncle Vince shrugged her hand off his shoulder. "Now, can we drop the interrogation?"

Shelli stiffened her back. "I'm just concerned about you, Uncle Vince, that's all." She turned in a huff and walked back to our little corner, but even I couldn't help wondering about that cough.

I looked over to check on Dad on the way back to our seats, but he wasn't sitting in his chair. I glanced around the room. When I couldn't see him, my heart throbbed — a strange constriction seizing my chest. I couldn't find him anywhere. His absence shouldn't have made me uncomfortable, but it did.

"Have you seen my dad?" I asked everyone in our hideaway. When Beth, Brian, Dane, and Shelli all shook their heads, I searched the room. "I'm going to look for him." I didn't understand the strange look of alarm Brian gave me. "With his unusually quiet behavior tonight, in light of his victory today, I wonder. I think I know why he's not celebrating, and I'm worried about his state of mind."

I checked the dining room and the kitchen, even though I'd just left there. I didn't find Dad in either of those rooms so I headed down the hall toward the first of the three downstairs bathrooms.

No one occupied any of them.

My feet stopped next at the bottom of the stairs. I looked up. Would he have gone up there to be alone? Granted, the whole house belonged to his brother-in-law, but the party and all the guests filled the rumpus room. No one usually went up into the actual house unless invited.

I climbed the stairs, listening for anything that broke the quiet above. At the top step, my ears perked at a disturbing sound. A hacking in the bathroom off the upstairs living room caught my attention. Walking to the door — the sound grew louder. If something made Dad cough that hard, he suffered from more than a sinus episode, like Uncle Vince.

At the bathroom door, I froze. The door sat ajar and through the crack I saw splatters of blood across the mirror. My eyes fell next on the handkerchief in Dad's hand and the red that already filled parts of it. I pushed the door open. Bent over, he hung onto the counter top with one hand while the other pressed the handkerchief to his lips. His coughed turned into gagging.

I rushed into the room and laid my hand on his back, not sure how I could help.

"I... I'll... be okay," Dad managed to say between gasps for air when the coughing stopped.

"I'll go get someone to help."

"No! No," he said pleading. He reached out and grabbed my arm. "Just help me clean this up and let's go home."

Nodding, I sat Dad down on the edge of the tub and took the handkerchief by a clean corner. I handed him a wad of toilet paper just in case he coughed up anything else. Under the sink, I found all the things I needed to clean the mess. Paper towels and window cleaner from inside the cabinet made easy work of the mirror, and, while looking for a can of cleanser to clean the sink with, I ran across a bottle of bleach. Filling the sink with water, I added some of the bleach, swabbed down the counter top and swished the cloth around the sink to remove the residue of red rivulets leading toward the drain. After locating the cleanser, I sprinkled it over the cloth and rubbed at the blood not washed away by the slow stream of cold water.

I turned feeling a touch on my arm and found myself staring at Brian in the doorway. The running water from the tap must have hidden the sound of his approaching footsteps, not that I would have hidden what I'd been doing. The expression on his face said it was too late for that, but he, too, struggled for words.

"Can I help?" he said, finding his voice.

"I need to get him home."

"I'll be alright." Dad rose to his feet.

Whirling around to face him, I lost my temper. "You will not be alright! From what I saw and cleaned up just now, you're sick, and it's more than a sinus infection or allergies like you've told me. Is Uncle Vince as sick as you? Are you both hiding something from the entire family?"

I don't know where my anger came from, but by the shock on both Dad's and Brian's faces, it took them off guard. I turned away and cleared all the paper towels into the trash can before pulling the liner out and tying it up. I couldn't look at either of them, so I didn't stop Brian when he helped Dad out of the bathroom. I kept gathering the cleaning supplies and put them away. Following the men down the stairs, I continued in my silent stewing.

Dad and Brian went into the party to make our apologies, but I didn't. I had no desire to speak to anyone.

They took their time gathering our coats and Beth but I still couldn't bear to look at Dad when they came into the hall. I stomped away, taking the trash out to the backyard through the downstairs kitchen. I came around the house and through the side-yard gate. My short-lived path of avoidance ended with them stepping out of the front door.

"What's going on? Why are we leaving so early?" Beth asked all the way to the car.

I wasn't ready to talk, and no one else answered her, either. She finally gave up and climbed into the back seat. She folded her arms and dug her chin into her chest, sulking.

Before I reached the driver's side door, Brian stopped me. "What's wrong? Why are you being so hard on him? Can't you see he's sick?"

Hurt and anger spilled out of my mouth without stopping anywhere near my brain. "I recently lost my mother, if you remember, and I haven't gotten over the grief of that, yet. Now, with what I just saw and cleaned up upstairs, there's a good chance that I'm about to lose my father, too. Why shouldn't I be angry?"

Brian pulled me into his arms and put his lips next to my ear. "I'll follow you back to your house."

The drive home remained a silent one. Brian, who beat us to the house, helped Dad out of the car under his constant protest. Beth ran ahead and unlocked the front door. I trailed them all across the lawn.

I called out to Beth. "Turn the porch light on so no one trips on the step."

Following Beth and Dad into the house, I half expected Brian to make his excuses and take off, but he didn't. He hung around while Beth and I put our things away. It actually worked out well. I wasn't ready for the answers to the questions I needed to ask Dad.

I made my way down the hall alone, on the pretext of putting my jacket away in my room. I wanted to use the phone, and I didn't want my conversation overheard. I needed to call Brother Donnelly—a doctor in my ward. I couldn't ask the questions I needed answers to with Dad nearby. And I didn't want to go into a conversation with Dad without at least an idea of what might be wrong with him. Behind my closed bedroom door, I picked up the phone and dialed.

CHAPTER
17

CONFESSIONS FROM THE HEART

*R*e-entering the living room after putting our things away, I listened in on Dad and Brian's conversation. "I know most of your family," Dad said, "and with the normal lifestyle they lead, you could never understand the compromises I had to make to live with a person like my wife."

"Papa!" Beth, sitting on the couch next to him, sat up straight and shifted to face him. "You can't talk about Nanie like that. She loved us. I know she did. I just won't let you guys keep saying these bad things about her. I know she wouldn't do anything to hurt any of us."

Dad reached out and took hold of Beth's hands. He wore his patient, teaching face, the one I remembered so well from all the upsets of my youth.

"Beth, your grandmother suffered from a sickness, and that sickness went all the way to her core. If she'd had a serious physical illness, we wouldn't have ignored it, would we?"

Beth shook her head with deliberate care.

"But we all tried to let her be," he said. "We tried to stay out of her way, and we were wrong. It only let her fall deeper into the pit of her addiction until it took over all aspects of her life. I came to see that when her actions shocked me enough to see the truth." He smiled at Beth. "But, by that time it was too late to stop her — to get her the help she needed. She'd grown too set in her ways to change.

"If you don't listen to the truth about her addiction, now, when will you? Are you satisfied to live in denial, like I did for

125

so long, for the rest of your life? I know what it's like to live a lie, and I didn't like it. I know that sometimes we choose to live in denial because it's the only way we can survive. I made up my mind that tonight I would make Brian understand the things about my wife that will explain her death." He stared deep into Beth's eyes. "You do appreciate this, don't you?"

She gave him a slow nod, full of reluctance, but her tears had stopped.

"Good. Now, sit there and let me finish my story." Rising and moving to sit on the rocker, closer to Brian, Dad made a weak effort to smile at me. "Anyway, as I said before, I lived a hard life with my wife, with her constant determination to have her way. Looking back, I don't think I ever could have taken the lead or even shared in the direction our marriage took. Not from the very start."

He glanced at me. "Did you know that I never actually asked your mother to marry me?"

What? My jaw dropped open. "Ah, no, no one ever told me that." There had to be more I didn't know.

"After my basic training at Great Lakes, the Navy assigned me to the hospital corpsman's school in San Diego. While in training there, they put me in charge of the squad of men in my barracks. Only one guy in my unit had trouble following orders, a real screw-up."

A faint smile of remembrance filled his face, but it didn't last long.

"After the third time I caught him screwing-up I put him on report. His response was to invite me to share a homemade meal at his mother's house in Los Angeles. It had been like an eternity since I'd been home to Michigan, and a home cooked meal sounded better than you could imagine. That's where your Uncle Joe introduced me to your mother. We started dating almost immediately. A month before Joe and I shipped out for Korea I asked your mother if I could give her a promise ring to wear. I told her I wanted to wait on any permanent plans until I returned from active duty.

"My last independent thought," he said under his breath.

"I never made another decision of my own for the next forty-some-odd years. She took the lead and set our wedding for three weeks later. We honeymooned in that large, three-story house her whole family shared on Newell Street, in Los Angeles. They gave us the entire basement floor for the week before Joe and I left for Korea."

My whole body ached seeing him hang his head in quiet reflection.

"I didn't understand until after my return from overseas just how much she loved to gamble." He looked up at Brian. "She told me once, after Annie's birth, that the thrill she got from gambling meant more to her than anything, even our new family.

"It's partially my fault. I should have recognized her habit as an addiction before she admitted it. By then, I was walking a beat in L.A., and had dealt with quite a great deal of people suffering from many different addictions. Once, after I went into traffic control, my partner—Roddenberry, I think it was—and I picked up a drunk in an alley off Wilshire Blvd. He'd sunk so far into his DT's he kept brushing imaginary bugs off his legs and arms. He even apologized for getting his demons all over the squad car.

"We took him to the receiving hospital, and I watched the doctor force a shot glass full of—I think—formaldehyde down his throat. He calmed right down, and the bugs went away."

Dad raised his hand and rubbed the back of his neck. "If only someone could stave off the craving for gambling so easily.

Wow! It was harder to be her husband than her daughter.

"You know, I watched my wife once at a Blackjack table on our first vacation here to Las Vegas in the early sixties. The look in her eyes reminded me of the starving refugees I'd seen in Korea. She wore the same expression as someone who hadn't eaten a real meal in weeks. I realized then, the high she got from gambling topped any feeling she could get from any drug or even sex."

He let out a deep sigh and remained lost in his thoughts. The silence dragged on so long I wondered if maybe he had tread into some extra difficult memories. My heart thumped in my ears. I wanted Brian to care, but he retained his business-like manner—

and it hurt.

"You were telling me about living with Connie," Brian said, urging Dad on and ignoring the darts from my eyes.

"It soon became clear that gambling consumed every aspect of my wife's life. She put it first, above everything. That may be why she did so well in business. She never feared over-extending herself. Maybe, the thrill of being on the edge, of winning big at business brought her close to her gambling high.

"But, like anyone whose happiness depends on nourishment from only one stimulant, it only took a short time before she needed a larger fix. After we moved to Las Vegas eight years ago, things became hopeless. I stood by her sometimes when she sat at one of those blasted poker machines. If she lost a round on the slot, she would console herself by picking up a handful of coins from the tray. She'd roll them around in the palm of her hand. Her eyes would glow as though she pinned everything on those new coins to be her next big win. I guess she only needed five or so to give her the adrenalin rush that fed those empty places inside her—you know, the places that even I couldn't fill, anymore.

"I didn't get to watch her very often, though. If she caught me watching her or even suspected that I might be hovering nearby, she would curse at me and tell me I was jinxing her. Near the end of her life, my wife grew more and more superstitious."

An unexpected sigh escaped my lips and Dad looked up.

His sad eyes rested on me before he studied the floor again. "It hurt to think I was the least of her priorities. But, I guess in her mind, anyone hovering over her specifically stood there to jinx her. More than once I marveled at how long she could play on those machines."

He glanced back up at me. "Your mother could sit there for hours at a time and never leave the stool. She didn't even crave food, anymore. I'm sure she received all the nourishment she needed from those damn machines—just from feeding the coins into the slot. In the last few years, she didn't need anything from anyone, not even me—except to drive her to a casino. And if it hadn't frightened her to drive a car through traffic, she wouldn't have needed me for anything."

"Then, why did you stay with her?" Brian said. "You could have divorced her and rid yourself of the problem. It's the only thing to do when there's no hope for a relationship."

"I made a commitment when I said *I do*, and I take my responsibilities very seriously. I couldn't just walk away from the life I had accepted when I married her, no matter how badly it turned out.

"Years ago, I looked for some kind of reason in our relationship. I came close to finding my purpose when I decided I would do my best to keep her from preying on the rest of the family. I couldn't let her keep stealing from them, but I wasn't always successful."

Dad focused on Brian and a wave of heat filled my chest, but I understood they shared a common background in law enforcement.

"For the first few years of our marriage, she needed me to support her and to share her dreams with. But after a while, our life changed. She isolated herself from anything that didn't support her addiction. And lately, her entire world lay in the few feet in either direction from whatever stool she sat on. A deep jealousy was the only real emotion she seemed to feel. That jealousy reared up every time anyone within her realm of slot machines won a jackpot instead of her. It galled her that *she* didn't get the rush from their win."

I couldn't believe it when Brian asked, "Didn't you ever try to reason with her or urge her to get help?"

"Have you ever tried to reason with a person who thinks it's the rest of the world that's perverted? She felt no obligation even to those she owed money. It got so bad that I hated answering the phone. Most of the time when it rang, the person on the line demanded the money we owed them. But, I think, in her mind everyone owed her. Even I had to empty my pockets for her all the time. Near the end, I couldn't even save money for food out of her winnings. That's why we ate so often here at Annie's. If we hadn't managed those apartments, I don't know where we would have lived. We'd have been in the streets.

"Don't talk like that." I bolted to my feet and ran to the rocker.

"You and Mom would have always had a place here."

"You know," he said, reaching up and locking his fingers with mine, "there's something I've never understood about your mother's family. They live as though anything that makes their life easier or fills some need for one of them is okay." He let go of my hand and looked away to the opposite end of the living room. "Even if it's not legal."

Dad focused his eyes on the dormant TV, just as checked out as the empty screen.

In the quiet that followed, I took a seat on the couch. Brian, looking through his notebook, surprised me. Had he slipped deeper into cop mode?

I watched Brian from the corner of my eye. "Is there a purpose to all this, Dad?"

Brian looked up from his notebook and answered for my father, who still stared at the dark TV screen. "Wayne wanted to explain why the family grief for Connie gives the outward appearance of being less than it should be. He also wanted me to understand how they could have as much fun at the party as they did tonight. We started out discussing some of the things I've uncovered concerning two of her brothers." He glanced in my direction. "I think he thought it a necessity that I know all this." His gaze centered back on Dad. "Because it embarrassed him that they had so much fun at his party, instead of still mourning Connie."

Dad, plugging back into reality, met Brian's stare head on. The two of them sat, not speaking. A strange kind of communication passed between them. Brian flashed him a strange look and closed his notebook.

I think I noticed a sixth sense in me just after I turned eight—a strange kind of tingling sensation in the back of my neck whenever trouble or danger presented itself. Watching Brian and my father exchange their fraternal look started an itch at the back of my neck. I reached back but couldn't touch the spot to rub the annoyance away. The tingling intensified. I wrapped my arms around me to ease the goose bumps rising on my skin.

A strange kind of fatigue hit me. I blinked and didn't think to open my eyes again. I gave in to the images filling my mind in quick, sporadic flashes.

Mom sat perched on the stool of one of her favorite slot machines, waving me away because I had disturbed her concentration.

I saw myself as a child, listening to one of the constant arguments between Mom and Dad. I watched from my usual place, cowering behind my partially open bedroom door.

My thoughts shifted again.

As a teenager, I stood by the ironing board again, cringing at Mom's screams.

I flinched and found myself standing behind Mom's chair, listening to a conversation at a family poker game. She and her brothers and sisters sat around the kitchen table in Aunt Sis's house in Huntington Beach, California.

I didn't have time to process this new image before it too changed.

I now stood at Beth's last birthday party. There was something different about Uncle Vince's and Uncle Dolly's hushed whisperings in the corner this time.

Was I hearing the part of their conversation about Brian coming to the party that I didn't hear then?

Uncle Vince turned away, but Uncle Dolly grabbed his arm and forced him around until they stood face to face again. He hissed orders within an inch of Uncle Vince's face.

Do I remember this from before? Is it something new? Is my mind filling in the blanks?

I forced my eyes open at hearing Dad stand. I scanned the room. No one had noticed my lapse into the daydream.

"I'm going to sleep now, unless we have anything else to discuss," Dad said, not much above a whisper. "I can't think of anything else I need to tell you — but, then, you know where I'll be if you think of anything you need to know."

Beth walked with him to his bedroom door. Before he turned the corner into his room, he looked back at us. I thought he might say something else, but he removed his hand from Beth's arm and disappeared. Beth's footsteps went on to the far end of the hall.

"What was that all about?"

Brian offered nothing.

"Did you ask him something that started him into that...that description of their relationship?"

"I asked him to explain his relationship with his wife."

"Is it important to your investigation to know how they got along?"

Again, Brian said nothing, biting his lower lip and staring at me. He thumbed the pages of his notebook without looking down.

I don't keep my fingernails very long, but my anger had the four of them digging into the palm of my hand. How dare he give me the silent treatment, after everything I'd shared with him. Worse, I had allowed my feelings for him to blossom. I could have struck out at the detective, instead I eased back, forcing my hand to release from its fist.

"Again, I'll ask — is my parents' relationship pertinent to your investigation?"

"It could be."

Can he think my Dad capable of murder? I stood. "Thank you for seeing us home. I think it's time for you to go."

CHAPTER
18

SEEING THINGS
IN A DIFFERENT LIGHT

*H*ow did I get here?
Uncle Dolly's house buzzed with mumbled, garbled conversations. Voices blurred behind all types of laughter, from small titters to loud, deep belly guffaws. I strained to understand just one of them, but the noise filling the room echoed in my ears — threatening to burst my head.

Most of the party guests were relatives I saw every day, like Nana, Shelli, Kathi, Lewie and my aunts and uncles that lived in Vegas. Here and there, though, sat friends and relations I hadn't seen in years.

I wandered around the room, catching bits and snitches of individual conversation against the rumbled background. Finally, I saw Aunt Sis and my cousin Annette in the corner, deep in discussion with someone. From the back, they looked very familiar. They didn't notice my approach, but once near her, I understood Aunt Sis's words perfectly.

"We all knew you were up to something."

The woman seated in front of them nodded. I watched the back of her salt-and-pepper haired head bob up and down. Again, the familiarity of that head struck me. I inched closer for a look at her face.

Aunt Marisa called out to the room about a new dish gracing the buffet table. The woman turned, keeping her back toward me. Everyone in the room held high-volume conversations with whoever sat farthest away from them, as always. Her silence here puzzled me.

I leaned in farther, my sole desire to have a glimpse of this woman's face.

Uncle Vince grabbed hold of my elbow and pulled me around to face him. "Let me tell you about my gardenias."

I stared at him while he spoke. Something about him didn't look quite right. His thinner frame stood a little straighter than I remembered. His hair seemed fuller, too. The crow's-feet around his eyes had smoothed out somehow. He looked younger than he had at Dad's celebration.

I cut off his rambling words about the flowers. "What have you done to yourself, Uncle Vince?" I asked, thinking he may have had some kind of quick-healing cosmetic surgery. "Have you seen a doctor?"

He threw his head back in laughter and walked away from me. Looking back over his shoulder, he called out, "Well, you only had to say you didn't want to hear about my flowers, and I wouldn't have come over." He stalked away without any sign of his usual limp.

I turned around to find Aunt Sis, Annette, and the mysterious lady gone. In their place sat two children around ten-years-old. A beautiful raven-haired girl sat in the lady's chair. A thin, timid boy in overalls and a light blue shirt stood facing her, hanging on her every word. He never took his eyes off the little girl, but she pretended to ignore him. The smile she flashed me said she owned the world. The glint in her eye challenging me to . . . Well, I wasn't sure what she challenged me to do, but her eyes twinkled like she knew she could have her every whim fulfilled.

The conversations around the room heightened, cutting through my head until it hurt. My mind couldn't settle on any of the snippets around me. Most of all, the little girl commanded my attention.

"Conchetta." The hot retort came from behind me, flavored with a strong Italian accent.

I whirled around. A vaguely familiar woman rushed toward me. She passed, never looking my direction. I followed her gaze back to the girl.

"I axed ya not t' bother anyone." The woman yanked on the child's arm, but the girl kept her eyes focused on me. She never gave the new woman more than a seconds worth of attention. "You were told t' just sit there, quiet 'til the train comes. Your Papa will not be pleased."

Something about the woman's accent rang in my ears. Her hair, pulled back in a severe bun, accentuated her long, slender nose, giving the rest of her Sicilian features a familiar look. Where had I met her? My gaze remained on the woman, wondering how distant this relative was to me.

"Have we met?" I asked, trying to catch her attention.

She shook her head, her long slender finger pointing back toward the children. But they had gone! Neither of them sat or stood by the chairs anymore.

"Annie, Annie. You should not be here. Do not listen to them. I will not let either of them tell you what they came here t' say."

The woman took my hand in hers, but the empty chairs held my attention. She patted my hand, Nana's soft reassuring words filling my ears.

"Annie, all will be okay."

I turned so fast the world spun. My eyes couldn't settle on any of the blurring figures that sat or stood around me. Not that it mattered, I only wanted to find the children again. But they weren't anywhere in the room.

The spinning quickened, forcing acrid bile up into my throat. Then, just as quickly as it started, the whirling stopped. Nana's comforting brown eyes and smoothing smile eased the tumbling sensation in my head and stomach the instant I recognized her. But where did she come from? I didn't remember the other woman letting go of my hand, but now, she, too, had gone. In her place stood my grandmother, Nana, stroking my fingers resting in her palm. She let go of my hand and reached up to touch my face.

Her hand inched its way toward my cheek. I longed to close my eyes and let her reassuring touch calm my uneasiness, but a giggle caught my attention. I jerked my head away to find the source of the sound.

Across the room, the boy and girl held hands, their skipping steps heading for the dining room. I took off to follow them, ignoring Nana's warning shouts. The soles of my shoes skidded across the ceramic tiles and I went down.

By the time I scrambled to my feet, I couldn't see the children anymore. A sinking feeling pulled on my chest. It grew, taking hold of every muscle until it hampered my efforts to breathe. If those children disappeared, how would I find out what they weren't supposed to tell me? A secret I just had to know.

Rushing through the dining room door, I stopped and looked around. The children weren't there, but in the sudden quiet surrounding me, a faint sound came from the kitchen. The little girl's voice chanted over and over again:

> When we grow up, we'll get married
> And you will do it all for me.

> When we grow up, we'll get married
> And you will do it all for me.

She kept repeating the rhyme in her rebellious, childish voice.

I reached the entrance to the kitchen in time to see her pulling the boy by his hand out the opposite door. I ran through the empty room where my aunt and uncle's staff worked, skidding and slipping on the tiles. But, again, the children were gone when I reached the other door.

At the bottom of the stairs, I looked up into the second-floor darkness above. I strained to listen, and there it was—the little girl's rhyme—so faint I nearly missed it.

The children had gone upstairs alone. Uncle Dolly would not be pleased.

The first step onto the stairs seemed higher than I remembered. With each foot I raised, the steps grew harder to reach. An ornamental buckle on the side of my shoe kept catching in the fibers of the carpet. Something didn't want me to reach the top. By the time I fought my way to the second floor, my breath wheezed in short gasps.

From the bathroom nearby the heavy footsteps of an adult echoed behind the closed door. I didn't hear the children anymore. *Are they hiding from me or is some other adult up here?*

The thunder of my heartbeat raced in my ears. I fought the urge to run away, to hide, but my mind would no longer be denied the answers it craved. My hands shook. The shaking intensified until my knees weakened, and I needed to sit. I reached out for the railing that looked out over the first floor. Unable to pull my gaze from the bathroom door, my fingers groped the air until I grasped the railing

The bathroom's door knob twisted, its slow-motion centering on every fear my imagination could conjure up. I clutched the wood tighter and covered my eyes with my other hand. Yet, no matter how I tried to block my view of that door, I couldn't.

The door popped from its latch and inched inward.

My view of the upstairs twisted, barely moving at first. The farther the door pulled inward, the faster the room whirled. Not until the door lay wide open did the spinning stop.

A man's shadow crawled out from the bathroom, projecting his full form on the rug outside the opening. I recoiled at an emerging hand but something held me captive. I couldn't go far.

The hand held a gun!

Everything around me teetered, yet the man's leg appeared — his foot touching the floor. An arm came into view next, then his chest — each reveal taunting me to keep watching. At his face, I forced my eyes to rise to meet his.

The room dimmed. The motion of the area took on a whole new frenzy. I had to get closer if I wanted to see his face, but how? I couldn't let go of the railing — the only thing keeping me upright.

The man closed the gap between, raising the shiny, black gun level with my chest.

I backed away, along the railing, until the floor gave way to the stairs behind me. The buckle of my shoe caught again in the carpet fibers. My quick steps pitched me off balance, my heel hanging over the edge of the step. The man with the gun reached out to me, but my quivering hands could not grab his.

Gravity took hold, pulling me down toward the first floor—backwards. Arms flailed, my eyes met his for only a fraction of a second.

It couldn't be... IT CAN'T BE...

I shot up from my pillow. The scream from my dream now a gasp for air. The faint glow off the streetlight on the next block sliced through the vertical blinds over my window. Little slivers of light on the opposite wall broke the oppressive darkness of my bedroom.

I reached over and turned on my bedside light. It may be childish, but I had to know that no one else stood in the room with me.

Throwing back the covers, I slid my feet into my slippers. My whole body still shook. Recounting the illusion of my dream though the ending had vanished.

Letting myself out in the dark hallway, I checked on Beth. She still lay asleep in her room across from mine. I tiptoed down the hall to Dad's room. My heart pounded against my chest. I reached into the bathroom and flipped on the switch, letting its soft glow light my way instead of the stronger light overhead in the hallway. Opening Dad's door, I peeked inside. His chest rose and fell for endless minutes until he coughed in his sleep and turned his back to me.

Even with everyone accounted for, the quiet house brought me little reassurance. *Why does his cough make me so uncomfortable?*

CHAPTER
19

DO I WANT TO KNOW MORE

*T*he next morning, with my heart racing, I walked down the corridor of Henderson's City Hall, on my way to the Police Department. Coming here might not be the best way to go about this, but I had to confront Brian. His tight-lipped attitude after Dad went to bed last night still troubled me. He refused to answer all but one of my questions. His lack of answers had gotten him kicked out of my house. But, with my anger receded, I needed to know why he thought of Dad as a suspect. My dream last night hadn't helped either, even now it nagged and urged me on.

I have to make him tell me something.

"I need to see Detective Brian Masters. Is he available?" I asked the Sergeant behind the five-foot-long front desk, meant to keep visitors from entering the rest of the room.

"What case is this regarding?" she asked without looking up.

"He's working on my mother's murder."

"Your mother's name?"

"Conchetta—Connie Easterly."

She turned to her computer and typed in a series of commands. The Sergeant picked up a pencil and jotted something down from the information listed on her screen.

Looking up at me she mumbled, "Just one moment please." Leaving her stool, she moved to a small office at the rear of the room.

Not long after, a young man, one who looked far too young to be a police officer, emerged. She handed him the piece of paper. He took off toward the rear corridor, his rubber soled shoes squeaking down the enclosed hallway.

"The internal phones are being worked on." She explained on her return to the desk. "You can have a seat over there."

My eyes followed her pointing finger to a bench near the wall, and I nodded. The sound of footsteps returning from the corridor kept me from following her directions.

Brian walked out with the young officer. He worked his way across the room to the reception desk but kept his eyes on the open file folder in his hand. Stopping at one of the three desks between him and where I stood, he closed and dropped off the folder. He held a short, hushed conversation with the lady there, and took his sweet time getting to the receptionist desk. He spoke to her before actually looking up at me.

"Ms. McBain?" he said. "How can I help you?"

His formal manner set me back. He had been in my home far too many times to act like this, but his attitude wasn't going to dissuade me. I pressed on. "Annie. Please, call me Annie, Detective Masters. I need to speak to you about your investigation into my mother's murder."

"As you should have inferred from our last conversation, I have nothing definite that I can share with you at the moment. We've had only a few breaks in the investigation, and I'm not ready to divulge that information publicly."

"Well, then we have a problem, because I'm not leaving here until I get some answers. From what you didn't tell me last night in my living room, I suspect there's a lot you have in that little notebook of yours that you're not sharing with anyone."

Brian's face tightened, and he avoided looking at the Desk Sergeant who sat there trying hard not to let her curiosity show. "If you'll come with me, then, we can go over what I can discuss with you in a more private place. I'm sure you don't want to talk about my findings out here."

I followed him to a small windowless room. Its dingy, dirty walls gave me the creeps. "Lovely conference room," I said searching the floor for anything ready to creep out from the corners. I pulled out one of the three chairs around the table, looked it over, and sat down.

"It's not used for conferences, but I'm sure you already know that. And, the condition of this portion of the building is the primary reason we've petitioned for a new, separate Police Department." He took the seat next to me instead of the one across the table, but still wouldn't let his eyes meet mine for more than an instant.

"How long are we going to play this game?" I said.

"What game?"

"The one where you hide who you think killed my mother."

Brian's eyes snapped up to meet mine full-on. His boldness didn't last long, though. Pulling his notebook from the breast pocket of his suit coat, he looked down and flipped through the pages with his thumb.

"I can't tell you everything, and before I share anything at all with you, you have to give me your word that it will go no further than this room — that you will not share what I'm about to say to any member of your family. I'm pretty sure that if you give me your word you won't break that trust. I'm only sharing things with you because of your father's relationship with my uncle."

He waited until I nodded my agreement.

"We still have nothing more on the partial of that slim tire print we found at the scene. There are no distinguishing marks on what we found, and it's a very common type of tire tread. It's a standard inexpensive tire sold at most of the tire stores around town under different brand names.

"There is one unusual thing that happened about a week ago while your family concentrated on Wayne's trial, though. I haven't yet connected it with this case, but my gut tells me it is. A young man found the grip — the handle — of a nine-millimeter over on Lake Mead Drive, out past the ice cream factory. While hiking, he slipped on some loose rocks, and in his slide down the side of a small rise, he unearthed the piece. It looked dirty, but new, so he brought it in and turned it over to the Department. We scoured the area and came up with a collapsible shovel, but nothing else."

I raised my eyebrows in surprise.

"No! In answer to that question you haven't asked, there were

141

no fingerprints on either. Whoever buried it either wore surgical gloves or knew how to clean up after themselves."

He fumbled through more pages.

"I've dug up more information on the credit card scheme Connie used to fund her gambling. I can tell you that the visitor you encountered in your garage the other night may be right, I think she carried the stolen card numbers for either a close friend or one or more members of her own family. It looks like she took the card numbers, for the person or persons who stole them, and handed them off to a mule for the purchaser. They got away with it for a very long time because they did it all by hand. They only used people familiar to them and avoided the Internet, or any other electronic transmissions. That's how they kept anyone from intercepting the information. They ran it as a 'Mom and Pop operation,' if you want to call it that, but it worked well for them."

He stopped and crossed his arms like I should be satisfied with the bits he had thrown on the table. But I wasn't that stupid. The dart of his gaze said he held something back, something much more important.

"I assume that Uncle Dolly and Uncle Vince are the ones you suspect of stealing those credit card numbers." I waited, but he made no effort to confirm or deny my guess. "Were you afraid I'd tell them if you said something to me?"

"I couldn't take the chance that you might let something slip to any member of your family. I've seen how close-knit and protective they are." He glanced at the notebook. "That is, when they want to be."

"I wouldn't have said anything, but I understand your caution. Now, tell me more about this gun handle and shovel you found, and why you think they're important to Mom's case."

"It's the handle to a nine-millimeter Ruger. The same caliber gun used to murder your mother. I think there's a good possibility it may be the handle of the gun that actually shot her. Even though we found no markings on it that identify it as the murder weapon," he said staring down at me, "my gut tells me it's connected. As for the shovel..." He shrugged. "I don't know. It looked pretty new. What makes it a suspicious item — we haven't found a store in Clark County that sells that type of shovel. I've even checked all the mail order and internet catalogues I can find. It's unique, and if I'm able to find where they're sold, I can find who purchased it."

"What makes you think these pieces are significant?" *I'm repeating myself, but I'll do it a thousand times until he tells me what I came for.*

Cocking his head and rubbing his brow, Brian shifted his gaze from the floor to stare into my eyes. "The person who committed your mother's murder has an uncanny understanding of police procedures. This suspect erased tire tracks, left no fingerprints or footprints at the scene, and used a very common type of handgun. He sterilized the scene so well that we found little or no evidence there.

"When we found no weapon at the scene, and no shell casings from the bullets, it disturbed me. Even since the initial investigation, I've had the nagging feeling that he must have disassembled the gun for disposal. He knew enough to avoid leaving anything we could use to identify him. He has, in my opinion, nearly pulled off the perfect crime.

"But, I do have a few things that I can't tell you about — things that have brought me to a conclusion I didn't want to come to. I need time to prove my suspicions before presenting them to my superiors — or to you."

The urge to retch gripped my throat, threatening to send acrid bile into my mouth. I had already sorted through my family and come up with suspects of my own.

"I think I came here today to see if we could connect the murder to whoever Mom delivered the card numbers to." The people using Mom for their credit card scam were the suspects I could live the most with for the crime. "At least, that's where listening to what you didn't mind telling me over the last few weeks has led my intuition." *The other growing suspect I couldn't bear considering too much.* "If you don't mind my asking, who are you centering your murder investigation around?"

I waited, but when he didn't answer, I gathered the courage

to venture forward.

"I know you're now looking harder at my family than you did at first. I need to know what you have in mind—if we are close to drawing the same conclusions."

His eyes widened for only a split second. I might not have noticed it if I hadn't gotten to know him better than the usual families he dealt with. At first, the closeness of our relatives and his willingness to share information made it easy to stay up on Brian's ideas about the case. Lately, though, he had drawn away, and suspecting who his probable suspects might be sent a shiver up my spine.

"You know I can't tell you who's on my suspect list." Again, he wouldn't meet my eyes. "But I can tell you my list isn't very long." His hand reached out but ended up veering to the table rather than touching my hand. My flinching had probably diverted him. "I think you have a pretty good idea who's on that list. That's why you came here today. Isn't it? If it makes you feel any better, both you and my Uncle Steve have pumped me for information this morning."

Now I couldn't meet his eyes. Why was this so hard? "I don't know about your uncle, but I came here today because I'm frustrated that this isn't solved yet. I know the longer a case stays unsolved the harder it is to pull together the evidence you need to solve it. I got the impression last night that you were still fishing around the family. My family? But I couldn't bring myself to ask you why. And—"

"And you wondered if I had anyone in particular in mind to build my case around."

We had both sidestepped the issue long enough. I couldn't leave here without knowing. I cocked my head and glanced at him from the corner of my eye. My heart pumped faster than I ever thought it could. "Is my father on that list?"

He raised his fist to his mouth and cleared his throat. Placing his closed notebook on the table, he covered it with his fist.

His silence told me what I'd come for. I stood and walked around his chair without saying a word. Not until I reached for the doorknob did he speak.

"Remember," Brian said, "you can't discuss what we talked about with any member of your family."

I nodded without turning around.

Walking through the building went by in blur until I found myself behind the steering wheel of my car, crying. Bits and pieces of last night's dream flashed behind my eyes. *Had I known from the beginning of my dream who the children were?*

I rested my head against the steering wheel, not wanting to accept what the dream had shown me. If only Brian hadn't confirmed it.

CHAPTER
20

THE BEGINNING OF THE END

*I*came back to the house around noon. Sitting in the driveway, I didn't see Dad's car. With my ruse for being gone so long no longer needed, sandwiches sat in vain on the seat next to me. I wasn't about to tell him I'd visited the police station.

I looked at the bag and my stomach turned. I wouldn't be eating any of it, even if it meant I'd wasted money. Dad was a suspect on Brian's list.

Shutting the motor off, I sat in the car with no desire to enter my home. For the first time since her murder, I allowed myself to think about Mom. I had always loved her even though she showed very little genuine maternal interest. Everyone in the family had accepted long ago that she lived her life to fulfill her own needs. With that acceptance, they allowed me to turn to them, and, most especially, to my father for parental comfort. Dad's genuine affection for me had always made him easier to love.

I remembered Dad splitting his support, love, and time between Mom and me. When I needed a woman's help I'd turned to Aunt Sis and Aunt Paul. I'm not sure at what age I realized the possessive axe Mom wielded over Dad gave her life, and, aside from gambling, its meaning. If it hadn't been for my Dad and the care and guidance of my two aunts, my childhood could have turned out so different.

The fear swirling in my chest would not be ignored. Starting in the pit of my stomach, it spread outward through my arms — my hands trembled. I gripped the wheel so hard my knuckles

147

turned white. The trembling spread upward, past my shoulders. When it reached my head, it settled into the back of my eyes. A burning sensation raged from the sockets. Moisture welled up to put out the fire blurring the closed garage door outside my windshield view.

My bursting lungs demanded air, and I gasped with the realization I'd held my breath.

I dropped my forehead to the steering wheel. The tears filling my eyes trickled out at first, but soon became a flood.

Sobs punctuated my anguish, fighting back images that filled my mind. None of my family could be involved in this murder. The credit card scam, I wouldn't put past them.

But – Murder?

I had to find out who had done this before Brian could make a case against my uncles, or my father. But how? I didn't know where else to look.

The flashing scenes crowding into my mind, slowed. I concentrated on the events of the night Mom disappeared. The uncles Brian suspected of masterminding the credit card scheme had helped us search for her until late that night, and even into the early morning. Both had driven separately to her favorite haunts, but then, so had Dad. Uncle Vince had been the first to come back to the house that night. But then it hit me that when Dad came in, he looked less harried than I expected.

Another round of shivers hit me. *Don't go there.* I pressed my hand to my forehead. *I can't have these ugly thoughts.*

What if Dad committed this horrible deed?

No! Don't think that way.

I remembered how Brian, a few days after the murder, mentioned a surprising lack of evidence. None of the family had ever volunteered the information about Uncle Vince working as an MP during his military service. Probably, because it would show that he, too, knew a great deal about policing a crime scene. And didn't Uncle Dolly work for a P.I. in Los Angeles as an investigator after leaving the Air Force?

They'd held that back, too.

The family did talk about Dad's police background with

Brian, though. Of course, because of Dad's association with Brian's uncle, that couldn't have been left out.

Could one of my uncles have killed my mother? Would the family protect one of them if they had? Is it possible that one or both of them could hide their feelings so well? Could they look me in the eyes and not show remorse over the deed?

No! I shook my head. *That's ludicrous! I have to stop looking the other way and get Brian's attention off Dad.*

I wiped at my eyes. The shadows near the top of the garage were gone. The afternoon sun shone full at the front of my house and it already streamed through the back windows of the car. It must be after two o'clock. I reached over for the bag of sandwiches. No warmth came from the foil covered sandwiches inside.

Pulling my keys from the ignition, I dropped them into my purse and picked it and the bag up. I'd sat there so long the muscles in my legs rebelled, but I forced them out of the car. Standing, I stretched my knotted muscles before walking around the front bumper and across the driveway. I deposited the bag of cold sandwiches into one of the trash cans on the far side of the garage and stood there with my hand on the lid.

Can I live with my uncles and wonder everyday not knowing? Could anything she did in her lifetime have justified this — execution?

For anyone of them to cover up a deed like this, every member of the family would have had to sanction it. This wasn't the same prank planned by kids who wanted to push their spoiled sister and her obsessive eight-year-old attitude off a train.

I took my hand from the trash can lid and headed for the front door. "I'm home!" I yelled entering the house. Had Beth come home while I sat in the car? It would be just like her not to bother me if she thought I was trying to work something out. "Is anyone here?"

I waited, but only my own voice echoed back at me from the empty rooms. The rest of the air released from my tense lungs in a long sigh. My purse landed in its usual place, on top of the curio cabinet beneath the entry hall clock. I sank onto the couch, grateful for the extra time to adjust before anyone else came home.

The grease frying my homemade onion rings popped. I dodged a hot projectile it spit at my arm and bent over to adjust the flame.

"Mom," Beth called, opening the front door. "I'm late 'cause I used the library after school for my report. Mom? Where are you? Oh, yeah, there's a man here to see you. I found him on the front porch."

I stepped back, looking around the fridge until I saw into the entry hall. Beth still held the door open. Just outside the screen, on the porch, stood a tall, stately man dressed in a gray suit. His bearing announced him as a professional man, but I steeled for a sales or political pitch, anyway.

"Just a minute." I turned the flame on the burner down to low, wiped my hands on the kitchen towel tied around my waist and headed for the door. "Beth," I said stopping next to her, "please, watch the stove."

I untied the makeshift apron and handed it to her.

"Can I help you?" I said after Beth put her purse and books on the love seat, grabbed the towel, and took off for the kitchen.

The man stuck out his hand for me to shake. "My name is Dr. Gamett, Dr. Brent Gamett. Are you Annie McBain, the daughter of Wayne Easterly?"

The pit of my stomach flipped and I covered it with my hand. *What now! Do I want to know?* "Yes." I sounded so timid I didn't recognize my own voice. "Why do you ask? How do you know my father?" *Wait, he had said doctor.* My heart jumped into my throat. "Has something happened to him?"

"May I come in? Your father is ill, and we need to discuss his illness."

A tingle swept over me until my knees threatened to buckle, but I managed to stand aside and let the doctor enter. After what I cleaned up in the bathroom at the party I should have seen this coming, but I hadn't. And I didn't want to face it alone. "Beth," I said calling out toward the kitchen, "call Uncle Dolly for me. Ask him to come over."

She nodded and headed down the hall to my room and a more private phone.

"Please, have a seat." I offered Dr. Gamett the couch.

He sat down so quiet I fought down a renewed bout of panic. I sat across from him on the rocker and waited, watching the slender man stare at his knees and wring his hands. I'd almost found the courage to ask him what he meant about Dad being sick when he spoke.

"I put your father in the hospital this afternoon." He looked up at me, his eyes almost apologetic.

"You did what? My father isn't sick," I said wanting so much to believe the lie. "If there had been an accident, Ron or some other policeman would have come to the house to let me know. You have to be talking about some other person. You can't mean *my* father."

The doctor sat up straight and rigid. "I diagnosed your father, Wayne Easterly, with lung cancer eleven and a half months ago."

Lung Cancer! The world around me tilted, again, but this wasn't a dream. How could he have kept this from me — and for eleven and half months.

"He refused to accept any type of aggressive treatment. I have seen him monthly since that diagnosis. I'm here today because the medication I prescribed for his cough and pain are no longer working. Lately, I've seen him weekly, and when he came to my office this morning, I found blood in his sputum during my exam. It concerned me, and I demanded that he be admitted to the hospital — immediately. I need to see how far the cancer has spread. And for the first time since his diagnosis, he didn't fight me."

CHAPTER
21

A FAMILY COUNCIL?

Uncle Vince arrived first — knocking at the door just a few minutes after Dr. Gamett dropped his bomb. His steps faltered, noticing the strange man sitting in my living room. Before I could introduce the two men, Aunt Sis and Nana came in with Shelli. Shelli took over the interrogation of the doctor, asking questions only a nurse would think to ask.

A few minutes later, with the three of them fully engrossed in the explanations of Dad's illness, Uncle Vince beckoned me into the kitchen with an abrupt tilt of his head. I followed him around the divider into the space between my kitchen and dining room. He grabbed my arm, pulling me back so no one in the living room could see us.

"How long have you known that Wayne was a patient of Dr. Gamett's?" he said keeping his voice to a whisper.

"I didn't know," I said, my voice normal.

He hushed me with a stern finger flying to his lips. I lowered my voice to match his covert nature. "I found out this afternoon when he showed up here. Evidently, he told Dad almost a year ago that he had lung cancer, and Dad refused any kind of real treatment. Why? Did you know Dad was sick?"

Uncle Vince didn't answer. He stared into the kitchen, and maybe for the first time ever, I saw how his mind worked. In those fleeting seconds with his guard down, I recognized the mechanics of a calculating intellect at work on a difficult problem. I had always suspected this uncle, who often played the bumbling buffoon to Uncle Dolly's conniving persona, was smarter than everyone thought.

Uncle Vince, his problem worked out, ignored my question and headed back to the living room. I wanted to follow him but my feet refused to move. No one in the family would believe what I had just seen in Uncle Vince. Why had he perpetrated such a lie for most of his life?

I made my way back into the huddle of people in the living room. From the moment I joined them, I lost track of everything around me. Absorbed in what Dr. Gamett told us I never noticed my house filling with people. My family just oozed out of the walls without my having any recollection of how the crowd grew so large.

I wanted to go to the hospital, but in their haste to support me, my family had blocked my car in the driveway. I didn't know how much more this day could dish out at me before I lost any resemblance of a sane person. But, Doctor Gamett, convinced me that Dad needed to settle in and finish the tests he had ordered. With his assurance, in time, I settled back on the couch. If I had to wait, I wanted to understand every word of Dad's diagnosis.

With each new arrival, the doctor stopped his explanations long enough to remind everyone that he had Dad's permission to discuss his disease with his family. He glanced at me. "I must confess, I never dreamed I would have to repeat this so many times."

Shelli hovered over us, probing the doctor with deeper and deeper questions. "Hey, take it down a notch," I said. "I'd like to understand what you are both talking about."

During their sometimes-whispered conversations, I discovered more about Dad's health than I really wanted to know. His cough, that I thought had intensified from the stress of Mom's murder, the recent charges brought against him, and, or the chronic sinus problems he had always suffered from, had worsened only because he was dying. He had refused to undergo aggressive treatment, telling Dr. Gamett he wanted to spare his family the anxiety of helping him through the side effects of chemotherapy. I couldn't help thinking, maybe Dad hadn't wanted to test Mom's loyalty.

If he had told her about the diagnosis, would she have put his needs first? Would she have set aside her insatiable appetite for gambling long enough to make him comfortable in his last few months?

I didn't think so—Dad probably knew she wouldn't.

"Did my father say why he didn't want my mother and me to know about his death sentence?" I asked, and the room hushed.

"Not at first. But after a few visits, we graduated into holding chat sessions when the exams ended. I've grown to like Wayne very much. I've never met a man with such a strong sense of loyalty. He never came right out and said so, but I gathered that his wife suffered from a classic obsessive-compulsive personality, and he didn't want her to know about his cancer." He paused to let the laughter and shouts of agreement die down before he continued. "And when I asked about his children, he said he wanted to share his time left without the sadness he foresaw if he admitted his illness."

He paused, and again, his eyes filled with that apologetic look. "From what he told me about your mother, Wayne believed that, no matter what, he had to stand by her. He just didn't feel that she would give him the same consideration." He leaned over and whispered just to me, "It sounded like he held himself responsible for letting her obsessions get out of hand. I could be mistaken but when he told me about her death, I thought I almost heard a sense of release in his voice—an out-from-under-it attitude surfaced in him. You are the one he regrets leaving. That is obvious."

He turned back to the others, and while I listened to him speak, I reached up to rub an annoying twitch at the corner of my eye. I laid the tip of my finger next to the moist corner of my eyelid. The rhythmic cadence under the skin stopped but returned when I released the pressure. After several tries to lift my finger, I left it there until I felt sure the twitch would not return.

"Annie," Aunt Carmen called from the kitchen, "where is your big skillet?"

"Leave Annie alone." Aunt Sis's tone scolding her. "Look in the stove. No, it's in the drawer under the oven."

I heard Aunt Carmen's hand slap the counter top. "I looked,

it isn't there."

Shelli laid a hand on my shoulder. "I'll take care of it." She apologized to Doctor Gamett before walking away. "I think those two particular aunts will get up from their death bed to cook for the family that comes to see them off."

I glanced down at my watch. Wow, only thirty minutes had gone by. I shivered. The thought of Dad alone in a cold hospital room brought on more distress than knowing what he'd gone through when they arrested him.

"Doctor Gamett, I don't know how much longer I can sit here and do nothing."

"You are not doing 'nothing.' You are helping me prepare all these people for another tragedy life has thrust at this family. I don't usually make home visits to prepare a family for what lies ahead, but this case is different. I have a great deal of respect for Wayne. He has shown a type of courage I rarely see in my patients. I think we came to know each other well enough that I can call him a friend. Just give him another half hour. By the time we arrive at the hospital, Wayne should be through with the tests I've ordered and back in his room."

Again—I saw that look.

"I'll even follow you over to the hospital, myself," he said patting me on the arm.

CHAPTER
22

FINDING DAD

*E*ntering the hospital, the dim twilight outside played on my senses. All the tears I shed on the drive over forced me to shield my eyes against the brighter lights of the waiting room. Its antiseptic smell offended my nostrils. The room's design did its best to welcome visitors in a gentle fashion, but just being here brought home my father's mortality.

I steeled against the murmured conversations. It hammered against my senses more than anything else in the waiting room. Those whispers made it hard to concentrate. They confused me more than the visions of last night's dream still shimmering in my mind's eye. I stopped and waited, with my hand on the back of an empty armchair.

Dr. Gamett joined me and touched my arm to urge me forward. Together, we walked through the rest of the lobby and into a long hall. Halfway down the corridor, I saw our destination — four elevators. Two sets of doors faced each other on each side of the hallway. He pushed the call button for our ride to the third floor — the cancer ward.

A thick silence hung between us that I had no desire to break. The set of elevators on our left broke into my concentration with a ding of its bell and its door sliding open.

The third floor, reserved for cancer patients and filled with their relatives, bustled with activity. Everyone wearing a hospital name badge nodded at Dr. Gamett. I stayed back by the waiting room chairs, letting him speak to the nurses at the desk.

"Take a seat," he said, returning to my side, "while I check on Wayne's progress."

He disappeared through a set of double doors leading to the patient rooms. I looked around at the empty chairs. So many to choose from, though none of them offered the kind of comfort I needed. I fell into the chair closest to the elevator but couldn't relax enough to let my back rest against the cushions.

Before long, people filled the couch across from me. I tried not to listen, but their quiet conversation sucked me in. The group of them, both standing and sitting, consoled the woman they surrounded. By the parts of the conversation I overheard, it became clear she had just received the news that her husband lay near death. She couldn't understand how the long months of chemo had failed him.

Would that same treatment have helped Dad any better than this unfortunate man?

She described his loss of hair, his inability to keep down food, the pain he had endured, and the progression of the illness under the drugs meant to kill the cancer. If this is what Dad had denied himself, I couldn't blame him. The thought of him bearing what the other man had suffered sickened me.

But, would it have given him more time?

I shifted my position on the chair and pressed my palms against my stomach to still the budding nausea.

I jumped under a sudden pressure of Doctor Gamett's hand on my shoulder. My hand flew to my mouth, but my muffled gasp still drew the attention of the others. I exchanged a nervous smile with the lady who sat inside her circle of concerned companions.

Dr. Gamett led the way through the open doors, into the cancer ward. I ignored the ever-present shiver I had suppressed over the last few months. This one originated at my shoulders and traveled downward, dying out somewhere around my knees.

I tried not to look into the open rooms we passed, but, like drivers who slow their cars to stare at accidents, I couldn't help myself. Most of the visitors inside the rooms looked back at me, their faces full of emotions. Their expressions telling me whether or not the patient inside lay near the end of his struggle.

At the closed door of Dad's room, I balked. *Can I go in there, look at his face and still hold back my anger at him for hiding this illness?*

Dr. Gamett's sad smile held such encouragement and compassion I found the strength I needed to open the door.

Inside, Dad slept alone in the four-bed ward. The bed sheet covered the bottom half of his body, but one of those awful gowns all hospitals make you wear covered most of his chest. An IV tube ran from a bag hanging on the pole attached to the headboard, dripping its clear liquid right into Dad's forearm. Other wires, attached to his chest, kept the gown from lying flat. They led to a machine monitoring the rest of his vitals.

My stomach jumped with every beat emitting from the machine. I took a step backward, only to collide with Dr. Gamett.

"I won't kid you," he whispered, "it's bad. Like I told everyone at the house, he has a small cell carcinoma—an aggressive, malignant type of cancer. The first symptoms are usually mistaken for smoker's cough, and since he told me he has smoked for most of his life, he could have had this for a very long time. It wasn't until he started spitting up blood that he came to see me."

I looked back at him, but never had to ask my question.

"Spitting up blood is common, but not to the extent he's experiencing it now."

"What causes him to bring up the blood?" I heard the words come out of my mouth, yet I stood there—afraid he would answer the question.

With a shift of weight from one foot to the other, Doctor Gamett settled into his professional mode. "Sputum becomes streaked with blood, when it passes over an ulcerated tumor. The tests we ran on Wayne today will tell us if the tumor has spread to the adjacent thoracic cavity and is possibly putting pressure on the surrounding nerves. If we're lucky, it hasn't invaded the chest wall, yet.

"There are only three treatments we use on patients in the same stages as your father. We can perform surgery if the tumor isn't too large. We also treat with radiation therapy or chemotherapy — all of which Wayne has refused to accept.

"What I'm most worried about now is a spot of pneumonia that's been found in his right lung. It showed up during our initial examination this morning."

"Why is that significant?"

"Well." He smiled at my confusion. "There are several things we look for to judge the depth of the disease. First, the patient may experience weakness. Second, they become anorexic or experience a sudden, unusual weight loss. And third, we have to deal with anemia — it's a deficiency in the oxygen-carrying material of the blood."

"I know what anemia is, Doc."

"Oh, good." He showed no sign of being offended at my shortness. "When all of these symptoms present themselves in the patient, the metabolism becomes balanced and their immunities drop severely. That's when they become susceptible to infection. Thus, they contract serious, non-related diseases — like pneumonia.

"As it stands, Wayne is in these final stages of the cancer. And I don't want him going through the strain of having his fever spiking over and over again, wearing him down even faster."

"I wouldn't like that either," Dad said, startling both Doctor Gamett and me. "I don't think I have much choice, but it would be nice just to die in my sleep."

"Dad," I said from behind clenched teeth, "how dare you talk like that." Tears rolled down my cheeks, and my words faltered on a sob that forced me to suck air deep into my lungs.

"How dare you have this hanging over your head and not let us help. Have I been a neglectful daughter? Do you care so little for me — for both Mom and me — that you would shut us out like this?"

He propped himself up against the bed on one elbow. "I kept you out of this because of how much you and Beth mean to me. I didn't want to live seeing the sadness you have in your eyes right now, every time you looked at me over my last few months. And, as for your mother—she could never have faced the possibility of my death. She couldn't have lived with it. So I chose not to tell her.

"That last argument you overheard was my attempt to set things straight. I couldn't die with my wife in dire trouble or live my last days with her under arrest." He dropped his eyes and whispered, "Or worse."

My shoulders quaked, a sob raking through my entire body. I stared at the floor, unable to look at him. How could he have hidden this from me—from Mom? She had died never knowing just because he decided she couldn't handle it—no, we couldn't handle it. How dare he! I side-stepped Doctor Gamett and bolted from the room.

Once outside, I collapsed against the wall. The tears came so fast and so thick I couldn't see the floor. I tried to shake off a gentle touch but it slid across my shoulder and, with a gentle tug, turned me around. Before I could form enough thought to do something about it, someone held me in a concerned embrace.

"Is it your husband, dear?" A tender voice asked.

"No." Another uncontrolled sob attacked. "My father."

"I think that might be just as bad," she said placing a tissue into my hand.

My one hand wiped at the flood of tears obscuring my sight, soaking the tissue. The other hand clung to my benefactor. Near collapse, I rested in her comforting arms until the sobs subsided. I pulled back and found myself looking into the moist eyes of the lady from the waiting room.

"Oh, I'm so sorry to burden you with this. Please, excuse my forwardness. I thought you were one of the nurses."

"Don't be silly, dear. I think I can actually understand better than most of the others on this floor. Do you want to talk? Maybe we can comfort each other."

Her eyes held the same kind of compassion that filled the doctor's and Lawana's. I gave in to the warm, comforting sensation spreading through my chest. There are times when you know that the Lord is close, and he has sent others to

161

comfort you. This was one of those times. This woman, in the midst of her own grief, had accepted the call to aid someone else — me. I could only try and do likewise.

"Yes, I'd like to talk to someone. As a matter of fact, I *need* to talk to someone."

She led the way out to the waiting room, sitting me down on the small couch in the corner. "My name is Doreen, Doreen Young. How long has your father been sick?"

"I don't know." That sounded weird, even to me and her puzzled look didn't help my shame. "He kept his illness to himself. We only found out today — and he's dying."

"Well, then he spared you months of agony by not knowing he was about to die. Didn't the chemo work for him, either?"

"He wouldn't let them use anything on him. He didn't want it. He gave up!"

"No, I'm sure he didn't give up. *I* made Harry go through the chemo. It was me that didn't give him any choice. I was *not* going to live on without him. And if there was any chance it would work, I needed it to. It's going to be hard to live with the knowledge of what I forced him to go through." She sat silent, staring at her hands folded in her lap before going on. "But none of it matters, I guess. When you're called home, you have to go."

My hand found its way onto her forearm. I couldn't find the words to express, but I understood exactly how she felt.

What if Mom sat before me in her place. How would she live her life without Dad? At least, I have Beth to lean on for a while.

This time I gathered her in my arms. We cried together for uncounted minutes.

Doctor Gamett, Uncle Dolly, and the Lamoreaux's entered the third floor waiting room at the same time, from different directions. I stood but didn't know who to greet first.

"Doreen!" Lawana said rushing forward and embracing my new friend. I guess an introduction wasn't necessary. "It's so good to see you after all this time. Thank you for taking care of my friend." She turned to me. "How are you holding up, Annie?"

"I think it was more like taking care of each other." Doreen reached over and squeezed my fingers. "Harry's chemo has failed. There isn't much time left."

"I'm so sorry." Lawana hugged her again. "We need to stop being strangers when our jobs together end."

The elevator bell rang and we all looked over to the wall of doors. Shelli and Brian stepped out into the waiting room. His presence brought back the reality of the ongoing murder investigation. I closed my eyes. *The Lord doesn't give you more than you can handle... The Lord doesn't give you more than you can handle...The Lord doesn't...*

"Annie," Doctor Gamett said, guiding me away from everyone. "Wayne really needs you, now. Can you manage it?"

"How long does he have?" More than ever before, I needed to know.

"The usual answer is three months or less, but—I have to tell you—he could slip into a coma and the final stages of his cancer any day now. We have to talk him into admitting himself into the hospice of his choice—and now.

"When we admitted him here this morning, he needed constant assistance with everything. I don't know how he has fared at home without you knowing. And, I just saw the results of the other tests I ran today—they are not good.

CHAPTER
23

THE HOSPICE

Settling Dad into his private quarters at the hospice turned out to be easier than I thought. The arrangement of the rooms gave a homey feel to the whole experience. Four patient apartments surrounded a full kitchen/living room section of the facility. Every patient's apartment resembled a sitting room with a bed on one wall and a private bath. It offered complete privacy for the patient and his or her family.

On the far wall of the common room rose two archways, one on each side of the kitchen unit. One arch and a short hallway led to the nurse's desk for that unit, where six nurses worked around the clock. The other arch led to an outside entrance.

Nowhere, except at the nurse's station, did this place resemble a hospital setting of any kind.

I walked into the kitchen for a can of juice I stored in the mini-fridge on the shelf designated for Dad. His first two days here had gone well. He rallied after his low at the hospital but remained weak. So weak Doctor Gamett didn't want him left by himself — not that the hospice or I would have done that.

I blinked at my hand hanging suspended in the air, stuck in the act of reaching for the juice. My thoughts had spaced out to nowhere again. Something I did more and more often over the last few days.

I shook myself and finished reaching for the can of juice I'd come after in the first place.

Entering his apartment, it looked like Dad had fallen asleep again. *Ugh, I really need to stop zoning out.* I didn't want to disturb him now, so I set the can of juice down as quiet as possible on his bedside table. I flinched when his eyes popped open.

"I thought you'd forgotten about the juice."

"No, I just got sidetracked. Aunt Sis called me on my cell." It wasn't a lie, but it wasn't the whole truth either. I straightened his covers. "She says she'll be back in about an hour. Nana's sending you some goodies she made this morning—some of your favorites."

"Oh, let me guess. I'm having fried eggplant and baked Ziti for lunch."

"You know her better than you should."

I walked to the window and stared out into the little garden filling the ground between Dad's window and one of the clustered units across the way. I studied the stepping stones weaving their path through the flowers, letting Dad drink his juice without me hovering.

"You know..." He paused so long I turned around to check on him. "...you really should go home. Since I'd planned to do this by myself, you can leave me alone. All this attention isn't good for me. And besides, Beth probably needs you right now. We're all still in mourning for your mother and I think it hit her even harder than anyone, except me."

"I can't argue that. But like I told you before, she's staying with the Lamoreaux's. And, according to my conversation with Lawana this morning, she's doing just fine." I put my hands on my hips. "And, right now, I don't much care what you want. I'm here, and I'm staying put."

We exchanged smiles until a rap on the door echoed through the room and broke our truce. I turned toward the door.

Brian waited until I gave him a guarded nod before he entered.

"Uncle Steve sends his good wishes," he said to Dad. "He asked me to check in personally and see how you're doing."

He sat in the overstuffed chair by the bed and I let them talk about Dad's illness and Brian's uncle. After a few minutes, he glanced up at me. "Annie, can I have a few minutes alone with Wayne?" he said, an unspoken apology filling his voice.

"Sure," I whispered, "I have to check with his nurse, anyway.

166

Do you want me to shut the door?"

"No, that won't be necessary. But, I do need to talk with Wayne in private."

I left them and headed for the couch in the common room. Halfway there, I turned toward the nurse's entrance and doubled back around. I shouldn't be eavesdropping. Brian had been polite in his request, but I had to know what was so urgent and private he needed to talk it over with Dad alone. I leaned against the wall just outside Dad's doorway where I could see their reflections in the stainless-steel door of the refrigerator.

The sound of Brian's rubber shoes squeaking against the tile floor filled the room. All that pacing drove me crazy, but jumping in there to do something about it would not go over well.

"Wayne..." He said standing in front of the window where a bird sat perched on the windowsill. "...I found where the shovel is sold." He turned to face Dad. "I also found only two sales made from that Canadian company to Clark County over the last two years. One came to a mailbox right here in Henderson, about six months ago. Is that when you decided to do it?"

Dad closed his eyes and sank farther into his pillow.

Brian made his way to the foot of the bed. "I've also found where you purchased a second handgun. About the same time that shovel arrived in Henderson, you purchased a nine-millimeter handgun — the same caliber that killed Connie. I need to know where that gun is, and I need to know, now."

Brian paced when no answer came.

Dad stirred and looked up at Brian. "I don't know where half my things are since I left the apartments. Check with John Derling, the new manager. He put a lot of our stuff in storage when he came in to replace my wife. But, Brian, do you think I'm capable of doing what you're suggesting? What, besides all this that sounds like circumstantial evidence, made you think I could?"

"I talked the possibility of your involvement over with my uncle. He didn't want to commit himself to an opinion. He did give me one piece of advice, though — "

"Let me guess," Dad said. "He told you to follow the evidence.

167

That it will never steer you wrong if you take it all into account. He also told you to follow it to its conclusion without tampering with it — or guiding it to where your intuition says it should go. Am I right?"

"You know you are. You taught him those principles. You told him that as members of the police force, in any investigation, we don't have the right to decide who committed the crime. You stressed to him that we must let the evidence solve the crime without involving our emotions. And heaven knows, I didn't want to come to this conclusion. I've tried everything I could not to end up here."

"How do you think Annie will take this if you charge me with her mother's murder?"

I caught my breath at the mention of my name. Had Brian considered at all what this did to me?

"I've seen the guarded looks you give my daughter. And, I know how detached a detective must stay in his investigations. Are you able to do that in this case?"

"None of that makes any difference," Brian said, his voice curt.

My heart plummeted. One of the many evils of eavesdropping — you find out how people really feel about you.

"I have followed the evidence. I grant you that it's, for now, all circumstantial. I wouldn't have confronted you with any of it except for your illness and the short time we have before us."

As a cop I know he has to do this, but must he sound so sarcastic?

"And you thought you'd come in here and tell me that you found these things, and I would just, what — confess to my wife's murder?"

"No." Brian gripped the footboard of the bed. "I didn't believe you would give me anything so easily. I had doubts early on in this investigation, when I discovered the subject of the arguments you had with Connie that night. I added that to the time during the search where no one can account for seeing you. And, when I factored in your ability to know exactly what we would look for at the crime scene. It didn't look good.

"But then, I found out that the shovel came here to Henderson, within the time frame that could fit the planning of this crime. I showed your picture to the proprietor of the Mail Boxes Etc. that hosted the address it came to. His ID wasn't conclusive, but he thought it might be you that rented the box. The more I dug, the more I came to only one conclusion. That you murdered your wife."

I covered my mouth to keep from crying out. *Oh Lord, please don't let it be true.* I loved my Dad. How would I ever bear it if he had actually done this to Mom?

"You, and what you taught my uncle, are the reasons for my being on the force," Brian said so low that I had to strain to hear the words, but I heard the pain in his tone so palpable I could almost forgive him for attacking Dad this way. "Not only did I learn my sense of right and wrong from church, I learned it from the two of you."

Dad pushed a button, raising the head of his bed. "I'm sorry if one of your heroes has developed the proverbial feet of clay. I can only give you the same advice I received from my trainer, and that I passed on to your rookie uncle a long time ago. Don't listen to or depend upon anyone else to set your feet on the path you know is right. Always—*always* let the evidence guide you to the proper conclusions. And, once you know you are right, don't let anyone influence you otherwise." He doubled over into a fit of coughing, but raised his hand when Brian moved to help him.

Once under control, he continued. "Don't let anyone sway your resolve unless he has more up-to-date evidence than you do. That bit of advice should govern your life as well as your investigations. I saw your uncle Steve use it in his decisions outside the job."

"I do use that and other bits of philosophy to govern both my investigations and my life. I don't think I prejudge any of the cases I'm assigned to. Do you think I wanted to come to this conclusion, here? I should have taken myself off this case. But after the evidence pointed to you, it was imperative that I make sure no one else took the straight course to the first suspect— you. It's an easy road to build your case without sifting through the evidence to see if there are others who could be responsible.

I have never worked by making the crime fit the suspect—and never will."

"Well," Dad whispered, "I can't make you change your mind, nor can I confirm your suspicions. You'll have to come to your own conclusions. As you can see," Dad said sweeping his arm around the room, "I have more pressing things to do right now."

Resting the back of my head against the wall, I gave in to an internal battle so loud that I didn't hear the squeak of Brian's shoes until he stopped just before he came through the door. I jumped up to leave the common room but didn't make it very far. Brian grabbed the upper portion of my arm.

"I figured you'd listen," He said. "I couldn't have confronted him if you had been in there." His gaze fell to the floor. "Do you want me to leave?"

"How could you treat my father like that. He couldn't—wouldn't hurt my mother."

He looked up at me. "Sure, Pollyanna, and the big bad wolf didn't eat grandma, either."

CHAPTER
24

THE CEMETERY

*T*he phone call came at 9:30 a.m., on the third morning of his stay in hospice. Beth had hurt herself in gym class, so Annie rushed off to take her to the doctor. Her leaving gave him the time he needed to put his plan into action.

He climbed out of bed and dressed in the shirt and pants he didn't let Annie take home when the hospice admitted him. He checked the pocket of his shirt. *It's still here.* Reaching out to steady himself on the door jamb he left the apartment and crossed the common-room to one of the archway entrances. From there, it wasn't far to the nurse's station. It took a great deal of effort, but he walked with a steady gait past the busy nurses and into the side room where volunteers gathered to sign in and receive their assignments for the day.

"I want to go to the cemetery," he said to the women gathered there. "Can one of you take me to my wife's grave?"

One of the women in the back stood up. "Are you able to leave the facility?"

"Yes, I am. I checked with the doctor and the on-duty nurse last night. Both of them okayed the trip as long as I had a family member or a volunteer with me. Since the school called my daughter away this morning to help my granddaughter, Beth, I thought I'd ask one of you to take me. It's just out at the Veterans Cemetery in Boulder City. That's where she's buried, and I don't know how much longer I'll be able to get around. I want to go there and say goodbye to her."

He leaned against the wall watching the volunteers huddled

in the corner. One emerged and headed toward him. He smiled. His plan just might work.

A Latino woman stopped before him and stuck out her hand. "I'm Deela. I'll take you to the cemetery. I just have to sign you out before we can leave. I also have to make sure there are no special instructions for your care off-site."

Deela pushed open the front door and stepped out before him. He basked in the first real sunshine he'd seen in several days. Standing still, he let the breeze surround his body, relishing in its freshness. *I'll miss the morning air the most.*

"We should go," Deela said, urging him out of the doorway. "They want you back here in two hours."

"Okay, that should give me plenty of time to say goodbye."

"Where is my father?" I asked the head nurse, Maureen, after finding his bed empty.

"Oh, Annie, I thought you went to take care of your daughter? Is she okay?" Maureen asked.

"It was just a slight twist of her ankle. By the time I arrived at the school, the swelling had gone down. The school nurse loaned her a pair of crutches and she went back to her class. But . . .where has my father gone?"

"Deela took him out to the cemetery for you."

"Deela?" I said. "Who is Deela, and what cemetery did she take him to?"

Maureen stared at me puzzled. "He said you had planned to take him to his wife's grave this morning. But because your daughter injured herself, he needed a ride from someone else. He asked for a volunteer to drive him out to the Veterans Cemetery in Boulder City. He said he had to do it this morning since he wasn't sure how much longer he had. They only left about three minutes ago. I'm surprised you didn't see them in the parking lot."

I pulled my cell out of my pocket and left the desk at a half run. Maureen called out to me, but I concentrated on dialing. I entered the common room to Dad's cluster of apartments when my cousin answered.

"Shelli," I said into the phone, "I need your help. Dad left the hospital. He had one of the volunteers from the hospice take him to Mom's grave."

"Why? After the funeral he never wanted to go there."

"I don't know why. I think something is going on with him. He never mentioned this to me, but the nurses here thought I was supposed to take him this morning. Can you or Kathi pick Beth up from school?"

"Sure."

"Good. It should only take me about twenty minutes to get to the cemetery, but I won't make it back before she gets out of school. I don't want her riding the bus with the ankle she hurt this morning."

"Do you think you'll miss them?"

"No, Maureen told me they only left a few minutes ago."

Pulling into an empty space in the cemetery parking lot, I stared out my driver's side window at a very familiar blue Saturn. How had Brian beat me here?

The walk from the lot to Mom's grave wasn't far. I rounded the corner of the office building, and there, across the sidewalks meandering through the plots, knelt Dad. The volunteer, Deela, sat on the bench a short way from him. It only took a moment longer to find Brian across the lawn, watching. I made my way across the grass, walking between the rows of flat headstones.

"Deela?" I asked, coming up behind the bench.

She faced me. "Are you Wayne's daughter?"

"Yes, I'm Annie McBain. Thank you for bringing him here, but I can see to it that he gets back okay."

"No, ma'am, I cannot leave a patient once I take him from the hospice. They wouldn't let me come back and volunteer anymore if I did."

"You can use my phone to call them for permission," Brian said reaching over her shoulder to hand her his cell phone.

How had he made-up the distance between us without me seeing him?

He smiled. "I told the hospice to call me immediately if Wayne left the premises. You can understand why I had to know if he went anywhere, don't you?"

I did not return his smile.

Deela took the offered phone and called in to the hospice. I listened to her relay the events of meeting us here and saw her nod her head as she accepted her orders.

"Okay," she said handing the phone back to Brian. "They said I can come back without him. You two are responsible for him as of now."

Deela rose and walked away shaking her head, no doubt wondering what she had gotten herself into. I could imagine the speculation among the volunteers when she returned. Would she complain about being dismissed without explanation?

I faced Brian, dismissing Deela from my thoughts. "Are you still accusing my father? Can't you let him die in peace?" My voice rose and the knot in my stomach tightened. "He already lives under a death sentence, one that he'll receive no reprieve from. You can't seriously want to prosecute him for her murder." I lowered my voice. "Brian, think about it. If he did kill his own wife, you can't get him in front of a judge before he dies. Besides, isn't he going to stand before the only judge that counts soon enough?"

Dad rose from his knees and stood over Mom's grave. It seemed strange to see his praying pose since he had never resorted to or relied on any type of faith before. Maybe imminent death had sent him searching for comfort from the Lord.

I started toward Dad, but Brian stopped me. "Let me talk to him first."

I opened my mouth to protest. He had no right to ask such a thing, but his expression held an intense pleading I couldn't ignore.

"Please, go stand by that tree," he said pointing his finger, "and listen."

I gave up on the struggle and nodded, letting him start off toward Dad, alone.

Dad never acknowledged my presence, but the tree I stood by

was so close it took no effort to hear their conversation.

"Wayne?" Brian said laying a hand on Dad's shoulder.

Dad didn't move. "I've been expecting you. Why did you wait so long to come over? Did you plan to wait for Annie?" He didn't pause long before going on. "I knew you'd alert the hospice, so I wasn't surprised to see you here when we arrived." Dad's shoulders slumped. "What do you need to know from me?"

"If you didn't kill Connie, what do you think happened the night she died?"

"The person who did this to her simply offered her a ride home... I guess. He probably didn't want to do it but had no choice." Dad turned but he still didn't fully face Brian. "He just couldn't let her go on using everything and everyone around her to feed that constant hunger she couldn't shake."

"There had to be a better way to handle it than killing her."

Dad looked straight at Brian. "You have no idea what it was like. She'd progressed way beyond caring how much she used people or what happened to them after she did. She pushed the limits with every family member, friend, or just plain acquaintance."

His voice dropped to a whisper, and I strained to hear him.

"Connie just never stopped. Once I found out about my cancer, I realized without me around, she would have no fences in her way. She didn't know about my illness, and, yet, when I tried to keep her from gambling by refusing to take her, for the first time ever, she went gambling without me. How could anyone let her go on without restraints? My wife would have either alienated her family completely or ended up in jail. And, contrary to everyone's thoughts, her addiction *would* have supported her after my death."

"Then, you did do this?" Brian said.

Dad turned back to the grave. "The actual act of shooting her would have been hard. But if he closed his eyes and squeezed the trigger, it would have been over in a second."

"Is that why you missed a little?" Brian's question made my knees threaten to buckle.

Dad went on without looking back at Brian. "The only thing

left to do would be to wipe out the evidence at the scene — dispose of anything that could incriminate the perpetrator of the crime. He couldn't leave anything, anywhere, to show his responsibility for the — execution. He'd only have about an hour to spare after that before he had to make it back to his humdrum little niche in life.

"That canyon where you found her would contain the noise of the shooting. Everyone goes there, to those desert coves in Henderson and behind that little campus of the Community College for target practice. I'm sure those canyons below Black Mountain contained the echo of his shots, as well as his victim's terrified screams."

"How do you know there were terrified screams?"

"Because I know my wife," Dad said glancing over his shoulder.

Had he looked at me? The emptiness of his eyes confused me.

"When she realized that she couldn't talk or bully her way out of what he threatened, she would have panicked. I can imagine how she screamed."

He lifted his hands to his ears and I flinched, wanting to do the same. If only I didn't have to hear it all.

"What else would the murderer have done," Brian said, urging Dad on.

"He would use a screen attached to his bumper to erase his tire tracks from the desert floor. He'd drive as slow as he could on that dirt road, to minimize the dust the screen would kick up.

"The only way out would take him back past where he left her body lying in the dirt, and down off that well-driven trail until he reached the pavement of College Drive. He couldn't stop and flip the screen back into his trunk until he reached that paved road."

Dad drew in a deeper breath than I had seen him take for a few days. His head dropped, and through my tears, I thought I saw him sway. I took a step, but stopped, gritting my teeth at the hand Brian held up toward me.

"Where would this man go next?"

"He'd drive down past the college, until the street met with Boulder Highway and head out into the pitch-black night of the desert filling the empty space between Henderson and the Railroad Pass.

"Keeping his speed under control, he'd go around the curve and pass the lights of the casino there. He'd slow to the posted fifty miles per hour. It wouldn't make sense for him to attract the attention of the Highway Patrol watching that stretch of road.

"The darkness closes in around you again after you leave that casino behind. But, he'd feel more than just the darkness of the night clouding his eyes. The dense gloom of his deed would shake him to his soul. With that deed, his career, his life, would be over—but, at least Connie couldn't hurt anyone else, anymore. From there on, his afterlife would fall into eternal damnation. That's what this deed has earned him."

Dad paused for so long I thought he had finished. I stepped away from the tree. I'd covered half the distance when he spoke again.

"There's no light out there, you know. I jerked the wheel to keep from hitting the sign for the turnoff to Searchlight and skidded into the dirt on the off-ramp. I drove slow in that pitch-blackness, watching for the stop sign at the end of the ramp. When I reached it, I stopped the car and pushed the mileage counter button back to all zeros.

"At that time of night, the only vehicles on the road are semis coming up from Arizona and California. Since there was no moon in the sky, I had to time the mileage out the way I had a few days before. So I drove on, watching the counter ticking away my progress in tenths of a mile. Those five miles from the off-ramp became fifty that night.

"After leaving the road, I turned the lights out. I couldn't chance anyone seeing me drive across the dry lake bed at that time of night."

"How did you know what direction to drive?" Brian said when Dad stopped again.

"I used the compass on the dash to guide me due west. A quarter mile across that densely packed sand I stopped the car. Before opening the car door, I reached into the backseat for that small folded shovel I bought out of Canada, I froze. Headlights lit the road I'd just left. I wondered if someone had seen me." He glanced over his shoulder at Brian. "Followed me."

Dad looked back down at Mom's grave. "I remember holding my breath for what seemed like hours. I held it until I recognized the lights belonged to one of those overnight truckers driving into or through Vegas. When I relaxed, I coughed the stale air out of my lungs.

"After the eighteen-wheeler disappeared, I undid the ties around the handle of that shovel and locked the sections into place. I took apart the gun that had killed her. I removed the slide then the barrel. I laid the receiver on my lap for a long moment before climbing out of the car. Dropping to my knees, I dug a hole in the hard-packed sand of that ancient lake bed. I felt for the edge of the hole in the dark and lowered the barrel, letting it drop inside. After I replaced the dirt and tamped it down, I retrieved the jug of water I kept in my trunk. With my hands, I felt around until I found the spot of earth where I had dug and doused the loose sand with the entire gallon of water. I then tamped it down hard with my hands. I knew that in the hot July air the water would evaporate quickly. I hoped that in the morning, when the sun hit the damp dirt, it would dry and blend in with the rest of the lake bed.

"I climbed back into the car and headed due east. From there, it was easy to retrace my steps and get back on the highway. This time, I headed for Boulder City. I knew the perfect place to throw one of the other pieces of the gun into a deeper part of the lake. It didn't matter which piece, because the barrel is the only one that could identify it as the murder weapon. I got rid of the screen there, too. Since there is no tidal action on the lake, I knew it wouldn't wash back up onto the shore.

"I buried the third part of the gun out on Lake Mead Drive, where that hiker found it — along with the shovel."

I couldn't take any more of this and went to my father's side.

"Do you hate me?" he said, tears filling his eyes.

"No." I glared at Brian. "I just don't understand how you could do this. You loved Mom."

"But Annie, that's why I had to do it. I couldn't let her go on hurting everyone when I realized my absence wouldn't slow down her abuse."

The ease of how he said those words froze my insides. I still didn't understand. I don't think I'll ever understand. How could I ever tell Beth?

Dad swayed against my hand resting on his arm. The pressure he exerted grew until his knees buckled. He collapsed over Mom's grave and closed his eyes.

I sat down beside him. Brian pulled out his cell phone. I eased Dad's head onto my lap listening to Brian call for help. Dad whispered to me and Brian touched my shoulder.

"What did he say?"

I glared up at Brian with mixed emotions. "My father said, 'Connie, forgive me.'"

CHAPTER
25

THE SOLUTION

I **stayed seated on the ground** long after the paramedics wheeled Dad across the lawn, my brain too numb to process anything more. Brian stood by the narrow service lane that ran through the cemetery helping them put the stretcher carrying Dad into the ambulance.

How strange this must look to people driving by to see an ambulance parked in a cemetery.

Deela climbed into the back with Dad. She had waited in the parking lot—never leaving her charge. Brian had convinced me to let her ride back to the hospice with Dad, so I waited in place.

The attentive paramedic who had assured me Dad still had time left, turned and waved back at me.

Brian helped the driver shut the two back doors of the ambulance and watched it drive away before heading back to where I sat. He reached down to offer me a hand up.

I placed my right hand in the grass behind me to steady myself and the ring on my little finger knocked against something hard. It couldn't have been a rock—it clinked-metal against metal.   I turned away from Brian's hand and ran my fingers through the grass over Mom's grave.

The picture of Dad kneeling before her headstone flashed through my mind. Could he have left something here? Did he want Mom to have something of his on her grave?

I pulled my hand back. Would disturbing it desecrate his offering? No, I had to know what he put here.

Again, I raked the grass with my fingers. Brian knelt next to me on the ground, but I didn't look at him. The urgency of finding what Dad might have brought here filled me. I couldn't stop—not even when Brian grabbed at my hand.

My fingernail hit the edge of a round, flat disk. The little disk didn't move so it had to be part of something bigger, pushed deep into the grass. I raked my fingers over the soil again, digging at the disk. It still wouldn't come up. I looked up at Brian, pleading for help.

Reaching across in front of me, he touched the piece of metal I had found. He scratched at it, too, but even he couldn't break it out. He took a slender folded knife from his pants pocket and opened it. Shoving the point of the blade into the grass beside the object, he lifted the disk from underneath. It came loose with a clump of grass.

A bullet casing, filled with dirt, fell out from the dug-up piece of sod. Brian let out a mournful sigh. "Do you know what this is?"

"No, but I'm sure you're going to tell me."

"It's the casing for a nine-millimeter bullet."

Brian rolled the three-quarter inch long, brass casing back and forth over his fingers. In quiet contemplation, he ignored the dirt that fell away from it. He reached down, and to my surprise, pushed the casing back into the hole it came from.

I didn't question why, I helped him tamp the dirt and grass back over the evidence that would solve his case. Once the ground looked more or less like it did before we started our treasure hunt, I sat there staring at the patched grass just below my mother's headstone.

"Well," Brian said laying his hand over mine, "now, we both have our answers. I'll have to tell my superiors about Dolly. Nana won't like it, but I can't let them continue their credit card scam. Anyway, since I know how well you can keep a secret, I'm going to tell you something I found out last night." His face took on a sheepish grin. "With his military police background, Vince has worked undercover for a special taskforce looking into a recent rash of identity theft. He's been working on it for some time now. They solicited his help when they stumbled onto that credit card scheme of Dolly's about a year ago. Vince has been helping the taskforce gather evidence against the entire lot ever since.

"It seems that he panicked when Doctor Gamett showed up at your house, because Gamett's seen him on his visits to the station a few times when he made his weekly reports. The good doctor is a golfing buddy of the Chief's, and, sometimes, he picks the Chief up for their Wednesday round. So, that'll have to go in my report."

What else will he put in that report? I raised my eyes to meet his. "And?"

"And what?" Brian stood, his hand extended out, offering to steady me as I rose from my knees. "I can't think of any other information I need in my report."

Was he telling me that the truth about Dad's deed would stay between us? I tried to let go of his hand but he pulled me into his arms. Brian held me close for what seemed like forever. The soft caress of his hand stroking my shoulder soothed the renewed quivers from my father's confession. I tightened my arms around his waist.

"My report has nothing to do with you," he said close to my ear. "I made my decision out of respect for a fellow officer, and because of that officer's importance to my own family. I don't agree with his solution, but I understand why he felt he had to do it. Prosecuting a dying man will accomplish nothing. And, besides, like you said earlier, he'll have to answer for his actions to a court higher sooner than I could get him into an Earthly courtroom. So, you don't have to feel obligated to me for anything." He pulled back and wiped at the tears on my cheeks with his thumbs. "My feelings for you have nothing to do with this case. They started a long, long time ago."

With my head resting on Brian's shoulder and the heels of my shoes sinking into the soft ground, I searched my heart for the desperation that had filled it over the last few months. This time, I found only hope.

AUTHOR'S NOTE:

You may not know after reading this story that it is a work of fiction based on the facts surrounding my mother's real gambling addiction. The idea to write this came about in a conversation I held with her a week before she died of stomach cancer in 1996. She requested that I tell the world how her gambling had ruined her life and the lives of those she loved.

After her death, I made fifteen or so attempts to put her factual story down on paper, but I knew my efforts had failed when each attempt bored even me. Since I know nothing about gambling, nor do I frequent casinos (even though I live in Clark County, Nevada), I could not base the story on anything that rang close to the truth of how her addiction led her life.

Staying true to her request, I incorporated how Mom's gambling affected my childhood our extended family, my father's employment as a Los Angeles Policeman, and the things I knew Mom did to finance her gambling. I could not speak for my brother so I omitted that I had one for the story.

I did fabricate the murder and the credit card scheme to give the tale depth. My friends at the Henderson Writers' Group suggested it would give the story more validity, and now with the finished product, I agree. It helped me to add a few red herrings for the sake of the mystery.

I feel I need to say that my father was a very gentle man.

He died from an Abdominal Aortic Aneurysm, Feb. 3, 2009. He never would have considered hurting anyone. He started on the Los Angeles Police Force (in 1948) as a beat cop, after leaving his naval service in World War II, where he served as a hospital corpsman. My father graduated the academy and, after walking a beat in downtown Los Angeles, he was assigned to a patrol car for traffic control.

I made everyone a little younger for the purpose of the story. Doing this allowed me to bring my grandmother, who died in 1978, into the book.

Similar to the novel, Dad never agreed with Mom's addiction, but had made a commitment to be her husband and tried to make the best of it. The bits he told about their courtship and marriage in the story were told in his own words. He lived after Mom died — surrounded by the few belongings Mom didn't gamble away in one of the bedrooms of my home in Henderson, Nevada, until his death.

Though I used the names of Mom's brothers and sisters, all of which are gone now, I did enhance a few of them for this tale. Aunt Sis and Nana are as they were in life. Shelli, Kathi and Lewie remain who they are, always.

Although a small amount of fabrication came about in the writing of this book in order to make it readable, almost everything is true. Mom's siblings did plan to throw her from the train on their weekly shopping trip from Newhall to L.A., sometime around her eighth birthday for the same reasons stated in the story. It *was* the favorite subject at every family gathering.

If Mom or any member of my family does not like the way I portrayed her problem, I apologize. Dad didn't seem to mind. When I told him about writing this as a mystery, he gave me his blessing. I received the impression he found it fun to be the bad guy for once.

In this story, I tried to show it, from a daughter's viewpoint. How, when a person's thoughts and actions are controlled by an addiction, life becomes complicated for everyone around them. How the people around them get in their way. And, how it can pervert everything they meant to hold dear. I realize my mom comes off as a dispassionate person in this book, but I know that, in her way, she loved us all. She was just not able to show that love until later in life. When I entered her room before the request to write this, she started our conversation with, 'I don't know why I never liked you, you're a really nice person.' I loved my mother and always sought to have her reciprocate those feelings. My five children adored her.

For the real story of her death, I have included the essay that aired on our local *NPR* radio station, KNPR, for their program Making Nevada Home series. It is titled, Just One More Thrill. For those interested in hearing the original, in my own voice, the essay is still listed at www.knpr.org, in the station's archives under the Making Nevada Home section. This essay offers a true picture of how Mom felt about life. It is not fiction in any way, and the events depicted happened exactly as written.

Just One More Thrill
**From Las Vegas' KNPR Radio Program:
Making Nevada Home
Aired: June 8, 1997**

I watched Mom dying through the open bedroom door. But, my cousin Annette's soothing voice held my attention. Mom and I never developed a close relationship, and since her doctor had diagnosed her with cancer, we didn't have the time to try. And, I don't know how I could have made it through the last three months without Annette's help.

At that moment, I couldn't bear to enter Mom's bedroom, but I couldn't bring myself to leave, either. I clung to the door jamb, my feet riveted to the floor, watching her life ebb away.

Annette brushed aside a lock of hair across Mom's forehead. While she spoke, I found it impossible to tear my eyes from mom's frail frame, dwarfed in the hospital bed the hospice had provided.

187

Mom, the ultimate steamroller, thrived on being the driving force in our lives. She may not have always taken us in the right direction, but people with an addiction rarely do. From as far back as I can remember, gambling had always been a malignant presence in our family. My earliest vacation memories came from trips to Las Vegas in the mid to late '50s, sitting around the pool at the original Thunderbird Hotel. Mom and Dad always came here to "bowl" with the Elks. We just stayed a lot longer than everyone else.

When my husband's job brought us to Clark County in 1978, it surprised me to find families living in the valley. But when I saw Henderson, it looked like a fine place to complete our family. Our problems began a few years later, when Mom and Dad followed us to Nevada.

Everything seemed okay at first. My parents secured a job managing apartments near UNLV. We didn't see much of them, but there came intermittent surprises, like the $800 television we received after one of her big wins. It wasn't until several years later, after we had secured the third or maybe the fourth loan to cover her gambling debts, that we realized she never should have moved from California.

When I think of my mother, I can't help remembering the old fable about the kid locked in the candy store. You know the one where the subject of the story gets sick because no one tells him he has to stop eating the candy. Well, we soon realized that Mom not only ate from the candy jars around her, she stole from everyone else's jar to fill hers.

This behavior went on for nearly ten years. Shortly after the fifth loan we took out for them, Dad showed up at my work. He begged me to help again—fifteen-hundred dollars this time. He said he couldn't stop her.

All I could do was stare at him. We were so far in debt there was nothing more we could do. I finally had to refuse.

That was the first time they packed up in the middle of the night to leave town. We discovered, later, that she had embezzled money from the apartments she and Dad were managing.

We panicked! Mom left us with all those unpaid loans we had

co-signed for. We nearly lost our home. Now, this was especially hard for me, because growing up, my family never lived in one place for more than a year. My brother and I sat down once and counted. We had actually lived in fourteen different houses and apartments in the four years I spent in high school.

We were also probably the only teenagers we knew with an intimate knowledge of how to file bankruptcy.

In the spring of 1993, I believe, was when everything fell apart. My mother had abruptly left town again while managing a complex of apartments on Tropicana. She hadn't bothered to tell anyone that she had gambled away over seven thousand, dollars of the rent money. This time her boss didn't write it off, he filed a criminal complaint. And without knowing this, they returned to town a year later. Dad tried to go back to work as a security guard at the Skyline Casino, in Henderson. He'd been a Los Angeles policeman for twelve years when I was young and had always regretted Mom's bankruptcies taking his job away. But this time, when Dad applied for his new sheriff's card, he promptly ended up in jail on the outstanding warrant filed by Mom's last boss.

Mom, whose warrant they couldn't find, tried to leave town by herself.

I lived with the stigma of an addicted mother all my life, but I never understood how bad her health was until we took her to a competent doctor who discovered her cancer. Mom knew I wrote, and that I hung on the verge of publication. It didn't profit her, so she never gave it much thought. But one day, after she couldn't get out of bed anymore, she called me into her room.

Her two requests shocked me!

First, Mom asked me to write her story and let others know how gambling had ruined her life. I reminded her that I wrote science fiction; that my ideas for stories came from the stars, space, and the possibilities available in an untouched future. If I didn't frequent the casinos, how could I write about her problem?

Over the next two hours, I sat awed by the detailed description she gave me of how she felt sitting at those poker machines. She described a type of hunger that she could never satisfy. It wasn't the winning she craved anymore, but the thrill that every quarter might bring the big jackpot. It didn't matter how many times she won; she just had to have that next thrill to satisfy her hunger.

Mom's second request stunned me, and my husband who stood at the door listening. She begged us to find a slot machine to put in her room. Her last coherent request was to die with her hand on those buttons. There was no mention of gathering her family around her, no remorse over the losses those machines had dealt our family, just a request to die with one in the room.

I stared at Mom, trying to feel something, anything while I counted the uneven heaving of her chest. "Only eight breaths in that minute," I said to Annette, just above a whisper.

Annette looked up at me. She had never stopped stroking Mom's limp hand.

While I listened to the tranquil sound of Annette's voice, I couldn't help wondering how we had gotten here so fast. How had this cancer, this stomach tumor that the ignorance of one incompetent doctor had missed until it was too late, taken Mom from her life's love so quickly? There had been only three short months from her new doctor's diagnosis to this, her imminent death from stomach cancer. But that other cancer she suffered from, her gambling addiction, will linger on in all our lives forever.

CPSIA information can be obtained
at www.ICGtesting.com
Printed in the USA
FFHW011934041118
49165658-53399FF